Judgement, Decision Making and Success in Sport

Judgement, Decision Making and Success in Sport

Michael Bar-Eli, Henning Plessner and Markus Raab

WILEY-BLACKWELL

A John Wiley & Sons, Ltd., Publication

This edition first published 2011
© 2011 John Wiley & Sons Ltd.

Wiley-Blackwell is an imprint of John Wiley & Sons, formed by the merger of Wiley's global Scientific, Technical and Medical business with Blackwell Publishing.

Registered Office
John Wiley & Sons Ltd, The Atrium, Southern Gate, Chichester, West Sussex, PO19 8SQ, UK

Editorial Offices
350 Main Street, Malden, MA 02148-5020, USA
9600 Garsington Road, Oxford, OX4 2DQ, UK
The Atrium, Southern Gate, Chichester, West Sussex, PO19 8SQ, UK

For details of our global editorial offices, for customer services, and for information about how to apply for permission to reuse the copyright material in this book please see our website at www.wiley.com/wiley-blackwell.

The right of Michael Bar-Eli, Henning Plessner and Markus Raab to be identified as the authors of this work has been asserted in accordance with the UK Copyright, Designs and Patents Act 1988.

Library of Congress Cataloging-in-Publication Data

Bar-Eli, Michael.
  Judgement, decision-making and success in sport / Michael Bar-Eli, Henning Plessner, Markus Raab.
    p. cm. – (W-B series in sport and exercise psychology ; 1)
  Includes bibliographical references and index.
  ISBN 978-0-470-69454-1 (hardback) – ISBN 978-0-470-69453-4 (paper)
  1. Sports–Psychological aspects. I. Plessner, Henning. II. Raab, Markus. III. Title.
  GV706.4.B355 2011
  796.01–dc22

                                                                                              2011009310

A catalogue record for this book is available from the British Library.

This book is published in the following electronic formats: ePDFs 9781119977049; Wiley Online Library 9781119977032; ePub 9781119976936; eMobi 9781119976943

Set in 12/15pt Times by Thomson Digital, Noida, India
Printed in Singapore by Ho Printing Singapore Pte Ltd

1   2011

Contents

Preface

It was in late summer 2007 – after a good day of windsurfing – when we came together in a nice restaurant at Flensburg harbour. Here we firstly elaborated on the idea of putting together a book on judgement and decision making in sport that comprises the entire up-to-date knowledge of this field. A field all three of us love to research. To be fair, we were more optimistic about the time schedule of this enterprise – none of us anticipated that it would take almost four years until we would finally hold the book in our hands. However, according to a recent theoretical approach to the evaluation of future events, construal level theory (Liberman and Trope, 2009), nobody would start big projects if he or she focuses on all the smaller or bigger hassles and efforts that immediately could get in his or her way (low level of construal). Instead, it is advisable to focus at least as much on the more abstract desirable goal in the far distance (high level of construal). In the end, we are very happy that we did not loose track despite various difficulties that came up during this time, for example, one of us changed his job position twice, and are able to present almost exactly the book that we had in mind when we met in Flensburg. We hope that it opens the door for many readers to currently one of the most interesting and growing research fields within sport psychology and that they will share our enthusiasm about its development.

The book has benefited from the help of many colleagues, who either contributed directly to the quality of one or more chapters or shared and discussed their ideas with us about judgement and decision making in sport on a more general level. Thus, many thanks go to Ralf Brand,

Vera Brümmer, Wolfgang Engel, Georg Froese, Thomas Haar, Thomas Heinen, Tanja Hohmann, Philipp Kaß, Sonja Kishinami, Jörn Köppen, Babett Lobinger, Clare MacMahon, Anne Milek, Alexandra Pizzera, Kirsten Pöschl, Rita de Oliveira, Geoffrey Schweizer, Christian Unkelbach, Kostas Velentzas, Pia Vinken, Karsten Werner, as well as to the performance psychology group at the Institute of Psychology at the German Sport University in Cologne and the students of the 'Judgement and Decision Making in Sport' seminar at the University of Leipzig. We also thank Corbis and Shutterstock for allowing us to use their images at the beginning of each chapter.

Finally, special thanks go to Karen Shield from Wiley who was of great support and never lost her passion with us.

On a personal level, Miki likes to dedicate this book to his son Asaph, with deepest love, Henning likes to thank Birgit for her love and support, and Markus likes to thank his wife Marei and his children Lukas, Mia, Emily, Bo and Leo for all their love.

Beer-Sheva, Heidelberg, Köln, January 2011
Miki, Henning and Markus

Judgement and Decision Making as a Topic of Sport Science

1

Judgement and Decision Making as a Topic of Sport Science

MAXIMIZATION AND OPTIMIZATION IN SPORT

Judgement and decision making (JDM) play a major role in *sport-related activities*, with the adequacy of JDM processes being directly related to success or failure in sport. For example, athletes have to continuously decide between alternative ways of acting during competition, and they must choose between means of performance enhancement which are either permitted or prohibited; coaches select players for their teams and decide on different training programmes and competition strategies; managers make investment decisions, dismiss unsuccessful coaches and evaluate competitors' success or failure; referees categorize game situations as being in line with the rules or not; journalists evaluate current performances and predict the outcome of future sport events – predictions which can be of major significance to spectators and fans who participate in the growing market of sport betting.

The basic metaphor often underlying these examples is that of a machine. In a classic book published almost two decades ago, Hoberman (1992) even conceived athletes in our society as 'mortal

Judgement, Decision Making and Success in Sport, First Edition.
M. Bar-Eli, H. Plessner and M. Raab.
© 2011 John Wiley & Sons, Ltd. Published 2011 by John Wiley & Sons, Ltd.

engines', which reflect the creation of 'men-machines' who attempt by all means to exceed the normal limits of speed and strength. Dissecting the modern Western sport establishments, Hoberman demonstrated how human science and industrial technology have transformed and dehumanized sport, with the emphasis placed on training and development, drug therapies and psychological research. In a more recent publication, Bar-Eli, Lowengart *et al.* (2006) referred to this machine-like metaphor, labelling its underlying principle 'maximization through optimization'. They argued that because the ultimate goal of athletes in elite sport is the maximization of their performance, this pursuit of success and excellence requires them to optimize everything – be it a movement, an arousal state or a decision to be made.

JDM HISTORY

The study of JDM can be traced back to the late 1940s, evidenced mainly by three major, quite independent approaches: the decision- and game-theoretical, the psychological and the social-psychological/sociological approaches. It has been generally assumed that, if individuals are involved in JDM, when engaged in choosing from among several alternative courses of action and if there is an understanding of how JDM processes work – be they related to spontaneous or deliberative decisions and if they are made under conditions of certainty, risk, or uncertainty (March and Simon, 1958; Simon, 1960) – it can increase the efficiency and effectiveness of the decisions. JDM has been studied since the 1940s by researchers from many disciplines. These scholars were especially attuned to the distinctive yet interrelated facets of the normative and descriptive characterizations of the JDM process (Over, 2004) with the implicit and/or explicit purpose of improving their outcome. In this sense, such an approach reflected the abovementioned 'maximization through optimization' principle (Bar-Eli, Lowengart *et al.*, 2006).

Standard normative JDM theories are based on postulates that enable one's optimal gain maximization and loss minimization (Baron, 2004). Despite the fact that the term 'rationality' has more than twenty different meanings applied in various disciplines (see Elster, 1991), instrumental rationality – which has to do with a person's effective application of means towards successful goal achievement (Weber, 1919/1946) – has become quite salient (Bar-Eli, Lurie and Breivik, 1999). For example, in economics, traditional theories assume that people have well-defined preferences and these can be represented by utility functions; people then maximize their utilities subject to budget constraints (Samuelson and Nordhaus, 2004). Such theories usually assert that economic agents are selfish and care only about their own well-being or the well-being of their household. When economic JDM behaviour takes place where uncertainty is present in the environment, maximizing utility is replaced by maximizing expected utility, using probabilities of the different future states. In short, the theory of rational choice used within economics embodies an instrumental conception of rationality, where the so-called 'homo economicus' is guided by instrumental rationality (Elster, 1989; Sudgen, 1991).

The inherent logic of the systematic approach outlined in such normative models led to the proposal of prescriptions intended to optimize human JDM behaviour. However, it soon turned out that real, living humans are rarely this thorough and precise in their actual JDM behaviour – a fact that was identified by Nobel laureate Herbert Simon (1955, 1960), who suggested the notion of 'bounded rationality'. This concept means that human rationality – when compared to any 'ideal' and/or normatively rational models – is bounded by limited cognitive information-processing ability, by factors such as imperfect information and time constraints, and, last but not least, by emotions. Together with Meehl's (1954) seminal work concerning the differences between statistical and clinical prediction, these ideas caused the area of JDM to become heavily 'psychologized', turning its major focus towards the description of real human JDM behaviour. As a result, JDM psychology has since then concentrated mainly on the gaps between the ideal and actual (i.e., normative and descriptive) facets of JDM in an attempt to understand their causes. Within this framework, it was repeatedly demonstrated that real JDM departs significantly from norms and prescriptions. As the different approaches to JDM reveal (see, e.g., Koehler and Harvey, 2004), JDM is currently conceptualized mainly in terms of human information processing and is regarded to a large extent as part of social and/or cognitive psychology (Goldstein and Hogarth, 1997).

It should be noted that the terms 'judgement' and 'decision making' are sometimes used quite interchangeably; for example, Drucker (1966, p. 143) – a leading management scholar – viewed a decision as 'a judgement … a choice between alternatives'. However, the current thought is that the two terms apply to different concepts: judgements refer to 'a set of evaluative and inferential processes that people have at their disposal and can draw on in the process of making decisions' (Koehler and Harvey, 2004, p. xv), with this process being considered as separate from the consequences of the decision itself. In contrast, decision making refers to the process of making a choice from a set of options, with the consequences of that choice being crucial. This broad distinction between 'J' and 'DM' should be borne in mind when the past trends in JDM research, as well as those in the present and future, are considered (Bar-Eli and Raab, 2006a).

THE DEVELOPMENT OF JDM RESEARCH IN SPORT

Most of the above work has not been reflected in either the 'micro' level of sport psychology (Bar-Eli and Raab, 2006a) or the 'macro' level of sport management (Slack and Parent, 2006), with the study of JDM in sport substantially lagging behind its potential. A seminal work in this area was an edited book by Straub and Williams (1984) – a collection of theoretical and applied book chapters on cognitive sport psychology. At that time, Gilovich (1984) stated that the world of sport was a potential laboratory for the study of cognitive processes associated with humans and, therefore, it was most appropriate for JDM research. Several years later, Ripoll (1991) edited a special issue on information processing and decision making in the *International Journal of Sport Psychology*, stating that the mechanisms dealt with in this special issue were concerned with the processes that intervene between the intake of information and the subsequent behavioural response (i.e., between the input and the output, which corresponds to one's 'software'). Accordingly, Ripoll (1991) focused on cognitive psychophysiology, priming, attention orientation, timing accuracy and decision time, anticipation and control in visually guided locomotion, semantic and sensorimotor visual function and visual search.

Another important publication in this area was Tenenbaum and Bar-Eli's (1993) chapter on DM, included in Singer, Murphy and Tennant's (1993) *Handbook of Research on Sport Psychology*. In line with Ripoll (1991), Tenenbaum and Bar-Eli (1993) discussed cognitive processes such as sensation and memory, short-term store, visual search, attention and concentration, anticipation, field dependence/independence, sport intelligence, problem solving and expertise. However, Tenenbaum and Bar-Eli (1993) also made a unique contribution *to sport psychology* through being among the first scholars in this area to discuss the possible disturbances and distortions in competitive DM, proposing Bayes's theorem (see Baron, 2004) as a normative model for coping with inefficient decision processes. Later, Tenenbaum and Bar-Eli (1995) systematically presented the Bayesian approach as a novel device for the advancement of sport psychology research, and conducted a series of studies using it to establish a crisis-related aid for decisions made during athletic competitions (for a review, see Bar-Eli, 1997). More recently, Bar-Eli and Tenenbaum (in press) presented the Bayesian approach of measuring competitive psychological crises in a new edited book – the *Handbook on Measurement in Sport and Exercise Psychology* (Tenenbaum, Eklund and Kamata, in press).

JDM in sport were further addressed by Tenenbaum (2003), who discussed highly skilled athletes' performances using the cognitive approach. He emphasized the stages of information processing which underlie JDM, proposing a conceptual scheme of accessing DM in open-skill sports, and describing several DM topics and their corresponding cognitive components. From an applied perspective, Tenenbaum and Lidor (2005) focused on how mechanisms, which determine the quality of JDM, are acquired and modified through deliberate practice and expertise development. These authors emphasized the important role played by visual attention in affecting anticipation; they also stressed the major significance of an efficient, interactive collaboration between knowledge structure and working memory. In addition, Tenenbaum and Lidor (2005) elaborated on the efficacy of cognitive strategies (e.g., attentional control, pre-performance routines and simulating training) by improving the quality of JDM in sport. More recently, Williams and Ward (2007) discussed DM as a derivative of anticipation processes.

As mentioned above, the study of JDM in sport has substantially lagged behind its potential – except for what we elsewhere called 'the Ripoll–Tenenbaum tradition' (see Bar-Eli and Raab, 2006a). This, for example, was quite surprising, because in 1985 one of the most provocative investigations in the history of JDM was published, namely, Gilovich, Vallone and Tversky's (1985) study on the 'hot hand' in basketball. This investigation was (one) part of the research programme on heuristics and biases (see, for review, Gilovich, Griffin and Kahneman, 2002), which culminated in the Nobel Prize being awarded to Daniel Kahneman in 2002. Gilovich, Vallone and Tversky (1985) showed how the use of the representativeness heuristic (Tversky and Kahneman, 1982) led to deficient perceptions of random occurrences during top-level athletic events (i.e., professional basketball games) and how such deeply rooted misconceptions can dominate human JDM behaviour. Their provocative findings inspired a great deal of research (see, for review, Bar-Eli, Avugos and Raab, 2006), but were generally disregarded in the sport and exercise psychology literature, despite their great theoretical and practical potential for advancing this discipline.

It could be observed that, in general, relatively minor attention was paid to JDM issues in the sport/exercise psychology literature until the middle of the first decade of the 2000s. This state of affairs was evident in sport/exercise psychology textbooks (e.g., Bakker, Whiting and van der Brug, 1990) and/or handbooks (e.g., Singer, Murphy and Tennant, 1993; Tenenbaum and Eklund, 2007) in which DM was treated – if at all – only negligibly, with the 'J' component as good as non-existent. To rectify this situation and to stimulate new theories, research and application in this area, Bar-Eli and Raab (2006b) initiated the publication of a special issue of the journal *Psychology and Exercise* in which they introduced different approaches to JDM that had not been sufficiently *related to* sport/exercise psychology and/or sport management up to that time. This thematic issue included eight articles – three in the 'J' and five in the 'DM' category. The articles on judgement were classified (i) by a theoretical approach, as either economics- or (social) psychology-based and (ii) by application, whether the subjects were judges and referees or other participants in the sport scene such as athletes, spectators, coaches, managers and bettors. The taxonomy of DM articles in this special issue was in fact an extended version of a matrix originally proposed by Townsend and Busemeyer (1995); DM articles were classified according to their (i) nature – deterministic (i.e., given a set of options, the one with the highest product of utility and expected success is always chosen), probabilistic (i.e., in most cases the option with the highest utility is chosen), or deterministic/probabilistic; and (ii) characterization – static (i.e., all options compared at one time), dynamic (i.e., where there is an interdependency of decisions or actions over time, with the time of their occurrence being crucial) or static/dynamic.

Bar-Eli and Raab (2006a) suggested that the taxonomical model used in their special issue (Bar-Eli and Raab, 2006b) could also be a useful approach for stimulating further JDM theory, research and application in sport and exercise. Indeed, in a more recent edited book on cognition and action in sport (Araújo, Ripoll and Raab, 2009), in which a section with six chapters on JDM was included, it was demonstrated by Bar-Eli and Raab (2009), who concisely reviewed the developments in this area, that this taxonomical model was indeed very useful. These authors pointed out a number of changes in progress that could inspire future research. First, the different approaches included in the JDM section of Araújo and colleagues' book represented the entire range of dimensions described above. In addition, a tendency could be observed according to which the theories and models derived from them were becoming increasingly dynamic and probabilistic. Second, a move towards integrating a number of different description levels in current theorizing and modelling was noted. Third, a number of theory-led applications of knowledge in the sports arena were revealed and direct cooperation with people in sports and their organizations was evident.

Bar-Eli and Raab (2009) felt that the broader theories of cognition and action were being applied far too slowly in sport, but that there were some instances in which this time lag was not as pronounced. In general, they believed that the developments in theories of decision-making processes were not quickly adopted by researchers in sport. Bar-Eli and Raab viewed this state of affairs as being unfortunate, because it is the nature of sport to involve both cognition and action. Therefore, they expected that JDM research, focusing on both what people decide and how they implement their decisions through movements, may come to play an important role in integrating research to be presented elsewhere in the future. In this book, we make an attempt to fulfil these expectations.

RATIONALE AND STRUCTURE OF THIS BOOK

As repeatedly stated by Bar-Eli and Raab (2006a, 2009), it was evident that although the analysis of JDM processes has received attention in different fields of psychology and management for quite a long time, JDM in sport has developed into an independent field of research only recently, with some excellent studies on JDM behaviour of athletes, coaches, referees and observers being published in the last several years, among others in Bar-Eli and Raab's (2006b) special issue and in Araújo, Ripoll and Raab's (2009) edited book. Today, JDM presents itself as an important topic in sport, but this fact is hardly reflected in current sport psychology and/or sport management textbooks or handbooks, as the above review demonstrated. The present book is meant to fill this gap by providing a general overview of JDM in sport. It introduces the fundamental approaches of JDM research in psychology and applies them directly to JDM problems in sport. Thus, this book offers a coherent basis for the study of JDM within both sport psychology and sport management, and by virtue of a specific compilation of interesting JDM phenomena, it can also be used as an essential reading for the study of general psychology and management.

Moreover, this book is also an important source of information for all those who are interested in the possible causes and reasons for success and failure in sport, for example, individuals and groups of people – researchers, lecturers, students and practitioners who are interested in psychology, management, sport psychology and behavioural aspects of sport management. It should be noted that studies on JDM in sport have recently been of interest to people engaged in behavioural economics and/or economic psychology. This is evident, for example, in Bar-Eli *et al.*'s (2007) recent study on penalty kicks in football published in the *Journal of Economic Psychology*. In addition, societies that might be interested in this book include, among others, JDM as well as sport psychology and/or sport management associations, and societies engaged in behavioural economics and/or economic psychology.

The first part of the book presents the basics of JDM. It begins with Chapter 2, which focuses on the most important 'J' theories, goes on with Chapter 3, which deals with the leading DM theories, and finally, discusses JDM expertise within this framework in Chapter 4. The second part of the book is arranged according to the different groups in whom JDM behaviour is analysed, that is, athletes (Chapter 5), coaches and managers (Chapter 6), referees (Chapter 7) and observers (Chapter 8). Each of these chapters includes a presentation of the specific JDM problems of that group, and follows with recommendations for dealing with these problems in practice. In fact, we hope that by applying these recommendations the performance of these groups can be maximized through the optimization of their JDM processes, without – to use Hoberman's (1992) conceptualization – causing any dehumanization whatsoever.

Theories of (Social) Judgement

2

Theories of (Social) Judgement

In a widely accepted operational way, judgement can be defined as the differentiation between different objects or identification of single objects in terms of certain qualitative or quantitative features (Eiser, 1990). In this basic sense, judgements are distinct psychological phenomena that do not need to be (but often are) connected with decisions (see Chapter 1, JDM history). Accordingly, most theories of judgement emphasize the appraisal of information and do not necessarily include assumptions about behavioural consequences (in contrast to theories of decision making, see Chapter 3). Typical judgement phenomena in sport are, for example, the evaluation of one's opponent's skill level, a coach's ranking of players, a referee's identification of foul play and a gymnastic judge's scoring of a routine.

The empirical study of human judgement can be traced back to at least the middle of the nineteenth century, when researchers tried to identify lawful relationships between the objective (i.e., physically measurable) magnitude or intensity of a stimulus and the subjective magnitude or intensity that people experience. This approach has been termed *psychophysics* and finds its classic expression in the famous Weber–Fechner law (see Chapter 2, Psychophysics). Since then, several different routes have been taken in psychology in order to reveal and understand the processes that underlie human judgement. This has led to the development of a few hundred theories with various

Judgement, Decision Making and Success in Sport, First Edition.
M. Bar-Eli, H. Plessner and M. Raab.
© 2011 John Wiley & Sons, Ltd. Published 2011 by John Wiley & Sons, Ltd.

degrees of specificity. Only a limited number of them has been used in research on sport behaviour so far. In the following, we will briefly describe the most influential lines of theoretical reasoning that have been applied to the analysis of judgement and decision making in sport.

PSYCHOPHYSICS

A common feature of psychophysical approaches is the explanation of human judgement in terms of basic laws of perception. Basic perceptual processes are of importance for the understanding of judgements in sport because they present the baseline on which higher inference processes may operate. For example, if a rugby referee's perceived information is already biased and he is not aware of this it is hardly surprising to find the final decision to be false. In this case, one does not need to assume additional biasing influences by intentions to favour a certain team ('motivated reasoning'; Kunda, 1990).

The already mentioned Weber–Fechner law is not only the first but also a prototypical psychophysical approach. It proposes that the detectability of any change in a stimulus (called the just noticeable difference) depends on its initial magnitude and that this relationship can be described with a simple logarithmic function (Eiser, 1990). For example, the higher the original intensity of a stimulus, the larger a change needs to be in order to be noticed. In addition, the law proposes that each just noticeable difference corresponds to a subjectively equal difference in sensation. When applied to the judgement of sport performance this could mean that differences between peak sport performances are much harder to detect by judges than the same differences between average performances. However, to our knowledge, such assumptions have not been considered in either corresponding research or in the development of judgement rules in sport. In general, psychophysical approaches have been applied in the field of judging sport performance only on rare occasions. We think this is a shortcoming of the field because these approaches bear some potential for the understanding of judgement and decision making in sport. Let us consider the following approaches that propose similar *lawful* processes of human judgement:

- *Range-frequency*. When people make categorical decisions on one dimension, they try to find a compromise between two tendencies: to use each category (the maximum range) and to fill each category to the same extent (Parducci, 1965; Parducci and Wedell, 1986). This basically means that people tend to distribute stimuli equally over all available categories even if the actual frequency distribution is skewed or some categories are absent. Unkelbach and Memmert (2008) demonstrate how this principle influences the decision making of football referees concerning the awarding of yellow cards (see Chapter 7, The tasks of referees).
- *Accentuation*. When people categorize stimuli into groups, they tend to minimize within-group differences and to exaggerate between-group differences (Tajfel and Wilkes, 1963). Together, this leads to clearer (less fuzzy) category perceptions than would be warranted on the basis of the actual stimuli features. For example, this contributes to differences in supporters' perception of their team in comparison to other teams (Hastorf and Cantril, 1954; see Chapter 8, Biases in judgements of sport performance).
- *Regression*. Judgements of frequency and probability have a regressive nature, which means high frequencies tend to be underestimated whereas low frequencies tend to be overestimated (Fiedler, 1996; Greene, 1984). Thus, regressing judgements to actual frequencies yields regression slopes smaller than one. For example, this may lead to the underestimation of players' success rates after peak performances (Taylor and Cuave, 1994; see Chapter 8, Biases in judgements of sport performance).

Judging sport performance aims mostly at the accurate differentiation between athletes and/or their performances. All of these approaches describe automatic processes that hinder a one-to-one correspondence between real (objective) and judged (subjective) differences. Instead, they predict systematic deviations from a perfect correspondence. As said before, these deviations should be kept in mind as the baseline on which other judgement processes may operate.

SOCIAL JUDGEMENT THEORY

Just as the psychophysical approach, the research on judgement – which can be summarized under the label of social judgement theory (Hammond *et al.*, 1975) – was inspired by an analogy between judgement and perception. Nowadays several slightly different approaches within social judgement theory exist, but they all derive from Brunswik's idea of probabilistic functionalism (Brunswik, 1955; Goldstein, 2004). The value of these approaches for the understanding of judgement and decision making in sport has only been recognized recently (Araújo and Davids, 2009; Araújo, Davids and Hristovski, 2006; Plessner, Schweizer, Brand and O'Hare, 2009).

According to Brunswik, people's ultimate goal, or *achievement* (Doherty and Kurz, 1996; Goldstein, 2004) depends on people's ability to perceive their respective environments as accurately as possible. The problem that arises with achievement is that people usually do not have direct access to the 'true state of the world' (called *distal variables* or *criteria*). They have to infer it from visible features of the environment (called *proximal variables* or *cues*). Importantly, these cues are equivocal and probabilistic in nature, meaning that their relations to both distal variables and their perceptions are not deterministic but expressed by correlations. These concepts are prominently illustrated in the Lens model (Brunswik, 1955; Doherty and Kurz, 1996; Goldstein, 2004).

The Brunswikian Lens model and the social judgement theory came to notable prominence particularly in the domain of medical judgement (Wigton, 1996). The main idea of the social judgement theory is that people have to judge certain *distal variables* or criteria (e.g., illness). Since they have no access to this variable itself, they have to rely on accessible *proximal variables* or *cues* instead (e.g., symptoms of the illness). These cues are correlated with the distal variable. As people learn the identity of the relevant cues and the relationships of the cues to the distal variables, the quality of their *judgement* improves (e.g., more correct diagnoses). This improvement is expressed by an ascending correlation (*achievement*) between distal variables and judgements. This correlation can be divided into several components, among these cue-criterion correlations (*ecological validities*) and cue-judgement correlations (*cue utilization coefficients*), thereby providing more comprehensive insight into human judgement than by investigating achievement only (Cooksey, 1996; Goldstein, 2004).

As with the psychophysical approach, we think that the potential of the social judgement theory for the understanding of judgement and decision making in sport has rather been underestimated so far. In Chapter 7, Improving referees' JDM, for example, we describe how a training programme for football referees can be developed based on this approach.

SOCIAL COGNITION

In parallel to the Brunswikian research, judgement became a core topic in social psychology after the Second World War when researchers intensified the study of processes that are involved in attitudes, persuasion, person perception, impression formation and causal attribution (Goldstein and Hogarth, 1997). Nowadays, these research areas are often summarized under the *social cognition* header. Social cognition research is concerned with the social knowledge and the cognitive processes that are involved when individuals construct their subjective reality; it is the study of how people make sense of other people and themselves (Fiske and Taylor, 2008; Kunda, 1999). Social cognition follows an information-processing framework and, thus, investigates how social information is perceived, encoded, transferred to and recalled from memory, and which processes are involved when people make judgements, attributions and decisions. Bless, Fiedler and Strack (2004) introduced a sequence of information processing as a

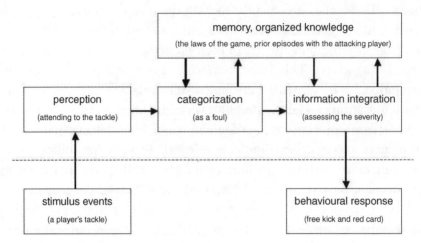

Figure 2.1   The sequence of social information processing applied to the example of a football referee's decision task (Bless, Fielder and Strack, 2004; Plessner and Haar, 2006).

framework for the analysis of social judgements (see Figure 2.1). It differentiates between several steps of information processing which link an observable input (e.g., a tackle in football) to a person's overt behaviour (e.g., a referee sending a player off the field). At first, a stimulus has to be perceived (e.g., the referee needs to attend to the tackle situation). Next, the perceived stimulus is encoded and given meaning (e.g., it is categorized as a forbidden attack on the opponent). Importantly, this second step relies heavily on prior knowledge (e.g., the referee must retrieve the decision criteria for forbidden tackles from memory). The encoded episode will be stored (automatically) in memory and may influence future judgements, just as retrieved episodic memories influence current processing (e.g., the referee remembers that the attacking player has been warned before). In a final step, the perceived and encoded information is put together with the retrieved memories and other information that is available or inferred, and is integrated into a judgement that is expressed as a decision (e.g., awarding a free kick and sending the attacking player off). In the following, we will briefly introduce three lines of research within the social cognition framework in which the body of work pertains mainly to judgements in sport.

Causal attribution

Causal attributions are judgements about the contribution of potential factors which led to certain outcomes (e.g., the answer to the question 'Why did I loose this game?'). The theory that guides most of the research on attributions in the field of sport is the attribution theory of achievement, motivation and emotion by Weiner (1985) which focuses, among others, on attribution processes in achievement contexts. Weiner's attribution theory offers general causal dimensions that may be used to categorize specific causal ascriptions. The causal ascriptions most common in achievement contexts following perceived success or failure are effort, ability, task difficulty and luck. They can be located in a dimensional space with locus of control, stability and controllability as the main dimension and globality and intentionality as two possible additional dimensions.

In addition to the attribution process and its outcome, the theory focuses on the emotional, motivational, and behavioural consequences of specific attributions. According to the theory, attributions will cause specific emotional reactions and influence future achievement expectations. For example, an athlete attributing success (failure) during a competition to an internal-stable cause – such as ability – will experience a boost (damage) in self-esteem, expects to be successful (unsuccessful) in the future and experiences feelings of hopefulness (hopelessness). These expectancies and emotional reactions, through their influence on motivation, will then jointly determine subsequent achievement behaviour such as effort in training sessions or partici-pation and actual performance in future competitions.

The assumptions of this theory have been widely tested in the field of sport and exercise psychology. Most of the findings are in line with the dimensional structure and the emotional, motivational and behavioural consequences as suggested by the theory (see Chapter 5, Judging one's own performance; Biddle, Hanrahan and Sellars, 2001; Rees, Ingledew and Hardy, 2005).

Impression formation

In general, the impressions people form of each other are important determinants of their subsequent interactions. Accordingly, processes of impression formation have a high impact on behaviour in sport settings. For example, there is plenty of anecdotic evidence that the way in which athletes form impressions of their opponents will affect their performance (Greenlees, 2007). Consequently, there is an increase of corresponding research on processes of impression formation in the sport domain in recent years.

Studies on person perception and impression started with the observation of order effects (Asch, 1946). In the classic paradigm, a person is presented with a series of adjectives that supposedly describes another person. A typical finding is that information presented earlier in the sequence has a stronger influence on people's impressions than later ones (*primacy effect*). There was much debate about the adequate explanation of primacy effects, which lead, among others, to the development of the *information integration theory* (Anderson, 1981). This theory mainly describes how people integrate information into a judgement by giving weight to various relevant information cues (*averaging*). Then again, researchers also obtained the opposite (*recency effect*) under some conditions, that is, a stronger influence of later information on people's final judgement. In an attempt to integrate the diverse research results, Hogarth and Einhorn (1992) developed the *belief-adjustment model*. It proposes that the direction of order effects depends on various factors, for example, the time when the judgement is formed (i.e., already during the processes of information sampling or after all information has been gathered). The value of this model for the understanding of impression formation processes in the sport domain has recently been acknowledged through a promising study by Greenlees *et al.* (2007). They studied the impact of the order in which information about a football player is received and found, among others, a more positive evaluation by coaches when they viewed the same video footage with a declining (successful to unsuccessful) performance pattern than with an ascending pattern.

Closely related to the debate about order effects is the more general question whether people form impressions in a bottom-up (data-driven) or top-down (schema-driven) manner. The latter perspective stems from social cognition's general assumption that social knowledge is organized in complex structures, such as categories, schema and scripts, and that these structures are interconnected in a so-called associative network (Bless, Fiedler and Strack, 2004). The knowledge that is applied when encoding a stimulus depends, for example, on its accessibility and applicability (Higgins, 1996). The accessibility of knowledge is affected by the recency and the frequency with which it or an associated structure has been used in the past; it can also be activated (primed) by environmental cues. A person schema contains information about the attributes of a specific type of person and the relationships among these attributes. Among others, schema can provide information about behaviours that are typically expected from a person of the corresponding category. This may be helpful in situations where only limited information about a person is available, but can also lead in the wrong direction if a person's attributes deviate from the expected ones. For example, the heading ability of a football player could be underestimated by his opponent because he categorized him as midfielder with rather weak heading abilities based on his playing position and body size.

The most prominent approach that tries to solve the debate between proponents of data-driven and schema-driven processing is the *continuum model of impression formation* (Fiske and Neuberg, 1990). It assumes that people use a broad range of processing strategies in dependence on a number of specific factors. For example, categorization processes may prevail when people enter into a social interaction, but they will rather apply data-driven processes if they are highly motivated to form an accurate impression and are in possession of sufficient attentional resources. This basic assumption that the application of different processing strategies depends on motivation and opportunity is prevalent in numerous so-called *dual-process* theories in social psychology (Chaiken and Trope, 1999).

Cognitive illusions

Social cognition's view on judgement processes has been shaped markedly by the seminal heuristics and biases approach (Gilovich, Griffin and Kahneman, 2002; Kahneman, Slovic and Tversky, 1982; also see Chapter 1, The development of JDM research in sport). According to this approach, people frequently rely on heuristics when dealing with uncertainty. Typically, they yield accurate judgements but also give rise to systematic errors. The most prominent are the all-purpose heuristics availability, representativeness, anchoring and adjustment. They can be described as the use of indirect methods in order to predict the criterion to be judged. For example, the ease by which instances come to mind may be used as a proxy variable to arrive at judgements about quantity. As such, heuristic-based judgements are constructed on the spot and, thus, are prone to reflect the properties of the judgement context that can lead in the wrong direction under certain circumstances.

Meanwhile, social cognition researchers have identified quite a large number of systematic errors (biases or cognitive illusions) in social judgements (for an overview, see Pohl, 2004). Given the assumption that judging sport performances follows the general principles of social judgements (e.g., Gilovich, 1984; Plessner and Haar, 2006), one can expect these biases to occur in the sport domain as well. The study of biases and their underlying processes can help to develop ideas about how accuracy in judgements of sport performances can be improved. However, as can be observed concerning the discussion of the hot hand belief (see Chapter 1, The development of JDM research in sport; Chapter 6, Managerial JDM; Chapter 8, Predictions and betting), biases can also develop an adaptive potential.

Although the empirical evidence that people rely at least sometimes on heuristics is overwhelming and the notion of capacity constraints seems to be self-evident, obtained errors and biases do not need to reflect shallow and mindless processing. They rather may result from over-generalized induction rules that are described in so-called *sampling approaches* (Fiedler and Juslin, 2005). For example, according to the cognitive-ecological sampling approach to social judgements (Fiedler, 2000), the quality of the stimulus input can sufficiently explain many judgement biases, such as illusory correlations and confirmation biases. This approach assumes that most judgements are based on samples of information that, for instance, are collected from the environment or from memory. These samples are almost never random and, therefore, may be biased in many different ways. It has been found for several judgement tasks that people lack the awareness (and the ability) to correct biased samples and therefore tend to base their judgements directly on the sampled information as if it was drawn randomly (Fiedler and Plessner, 2009). Likewise, many social cognition theories assume that judgements are based on and biased by information that has been made selectively accessible (e.g., Mussweiler, 2003; Mussweiler and Strack, 1999). Accordingly, Unkelbach and Plessner (2008) provide an example of how the assessment of a football player's qualities can be biased due to the selective activation of memory contents (see Chapter 8, Biases in judgements of sport performance).

Together, sampling approaches highlight that judgement biases can often result from unbiased cognitive operations applied to a biased stimulus samples. This initial sampling bias may not reflect the judge's own selective memory but the selective manner in which the environment supplies judges with relevant information. For instance, larger samples are supplied about oneself than about others, or about one's own in-group than others (Fiedler and Walther, 2004). Accordingly, judgements often exhibit a self-serving bias or in-group-serving bias without people being *motivated* to bias their judgement.

Nevertheless, it is important to note that a large amount of research on social judgement also emphasizes the role of motivational and emotional processes in the emergence of social judgements (Kunda, 1990, 1999). This may be even more the case in the domain of sport, where team membership, supporters, wins and losses, and the corresponding feelings play a major role.

SUMMARY

The study of human judgement has a long tradition in experimental psychology that led to the development of a large number of different paradigms and theories. Our introduction covers a few important lines of research within this field, which are of great significance for the study of judgement and decision processes in sport. In general, their explanatory power for the understanding of sport behaviour has rather been undervalued so far. However, we will provide some promising examples of research in the sport domain that explicitly refer to these approaches in the following chapters.

THEORY APPLICATION

Example: Imagine two opposing football players who go for the ball in the penalty area. The defender correctly tackles the striker who falls to the ground. The referee awards a penalty. Which processes would different theoretical perspectives focus on in order to find an explanation for this wrong decision?

Social judgement theory: From this perspective it would be of main importance to understand which cues have been used by the referee and how. For example, did she use only relevant cues, such as the defender's touching of the ball, or also irrelevant cues, such as the crowd noise? In addition, one would try to find out how good the referee actually is at using the relevant cues. Does she correctly take into account the probabilistic relationships between the observable cues and foul play, as well as possible cue interactions?

Social cognition: Several routes can be taken from a social cognition perspective in order to explain the referee's decision. For example, one could analyse the referee's causal attribution. Did the striker fall because the defender hit her, because she was exhausted, or because she tried to deceive the referee? Another approach could focus on the referee's prior knowledge about the players. Perhaps, she learned before that the defender's team has an aggressive reputation. Finally, one could ask if she recognized the striker as an in-group member and wanted to favour her.

Theories of Decision Making

3

Theories of Decision Making

The number of theories in decision making naturally depends on the broadness of the definition of what it means to make a decision. If we consider descriptive preference theories in the domains of judgement, decision making, reasoning, risk perception and behavioural finance, nearly 300 theories have been counted (see lists on www.muellerscience.com). These theories describe decision making at the behavioural, computational and neurophysiologic level (see Figure 3.1). However, if we look only at behavioural theories used in sport-related applications, then we can easily reduce the number to about a dozen. These dozen theories represent a good selection of theories that can be applied to judgement and decision making in sport. However, as we will argue the improvement of the field can be faster if we use developments of psychological and economic theories to test them in sport and in some cases may develop our own models that fit the specific conditions on fast and dynamic choices in the world of sport. Because we will concentrate on theories of decision making used exclusively in sport, we will focus on these latter cases in more detail.

Decision-making theories in sport can be classified according to (i) their nature (deterministic, probabilistic or deterministic/probabilistic) and (ii) their timeline: static (i.e., all options compared at one time), dynamic (a sample of options is considered in sequential sampling)

Judgement, Decision Making and Success in Sport, First Edition.
M. Bar-Eli, H. Plessner and M. Raab.

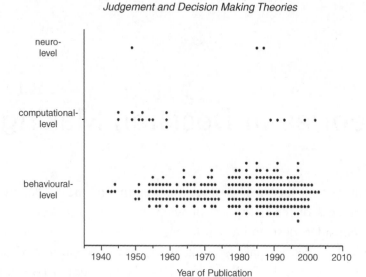

Judgement and Decision Making Theories

Figure 3.1 Historical distribution of theories of decision making based on three levels of description: behavioural level, computational level, and neurophysiologic level. Each point represents a JDM theory.

or static/dynamic (see Chapter 1, The development of JDM research in sport). In this book we will add yet another dimension, that is, 'time of theory development'. We are particularly interested in the progress of decision-making theories over the past decades, and specifically in the delay between the development of such theories in psychology or economics and their application in sport. This is an informative exercise because it provides a 'snapshot' of changes in this field.

Figure 3.2 shows how these theories are distributed over the dimensions of nature and characterization with time as the third dimension. The line between two theories reflects the original publication of the theory in the social sciences and its use by researchers in sport science. As is evident in Figure 3.2, the delay is impressive.

Let us consider some of the theories displayed in Figure 3.2 in more detail. We will restrict that overview to decision-making theories focusing on fast choices mainly prominent to athletes that have limited time to choose. In Chapter 6 we will introduce more rational theories such as Bayes theory because they apply specifically to choices of

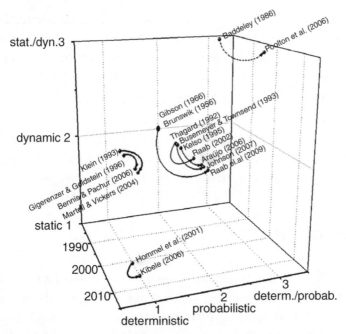

Figure 3.2 Theories of decision making used in sports plotted by three dimensions: nature, characterization, and time of theory development. Thick lines represent theories that are deterministic, thin lines represent theories that are probabilistic and dotted lines represent theories that are both deterministic and probabilistic.

managers and coaches where both are often confronted with decisions that can be preplanned.

SUBJECTIVE EXPECTED UTILITY THEORY

A famous and historical example of a static and deterministic theory is Edwards's (1954) subjective expected utility (SEU) theory, which in turn was extended by Kahneman and Tversky (1979) to become their prospect theory (see below). SEU has two main parameters: 'uncertainty', that is, the probability of success, and 'utility', that is, the value of the chosen option. The product of these two parameters is calculated and the option with the highest outcome is chosen. Consider a simple case of a basketball player who has at some point in the game two options, such as shooting to the basket (high value to directly score) or passing to a teammate (lower value to directly score). The probability of success is, for instance, a matter of the distance to the basket such that the nearer the player is to the basket, the higher the chance of a hit. This is called subjective utility theory because the utility of hitting is subjective, such that an NBA three-point shooting contest winner has a higher probability of hitting a basket from various distances compared to most readers of this chapter. A problem with SEU is that people do not always choose the option with the highest subjective utility.

PROSPECT THEORY

In contrast to SEU, prospect theory takes other factors, such as previous outcome of choices, into account. Prospect theory assumes two phases: (i) the editing of the problem at hand, such that information is encoded, transformed and mentally represented, and (ii) the evaluation of options. Editing is defined through four mechanisms: combination of options (e.g., combining options with the same consequence), simplification (e.g., rounding probabilities up or down for direct comparison), segregation (e.g., separating options with high and low probability of success) and elimination (e.g., excluding one option that does not possess a specific attribute and then further comparing the remaining options). These four editing mechanisms result in various possible options to be considered so that at the end a selected number of options will be evaluated based on a winning or losing situation (see cumulative prospect theory in Tversky and Kahneman, 1992; see also Johnson, 2008).

Prospect theory predicts that people, for instance, in a casino, play riskier options when they are in a losing situation and make less risky decisions in a winning situation. However, in sport we can explore other behaviours. For instance, in basketball, it may make sense for teams to take more risks when they are winning, because it does not matter by how much you win, whereas in a casino it does matter how much you win. Both these theories, subjective utility theory and prospect theory, are static and deterministic and therefore could not describe choices in rapidly changing environments. Likewise, a playmaker in basketball cannot pass each ball to the player with the highest probability of success as the defence can adjust easily to such an allocation behaviour. In sport, therefore, probabilistic and dynamic theories became more prominent over the last decades.

DECISIONAL FIELD THEORY

Let us consider a dynamic and probabilistic model that extends the SEU model as an alternative description: Busemeyer and Townsend's (1993) decision field theory (DFT). DFT adds the temporal dimension to the SEU model. One central assumption is that the preference for options fluctuates over time. Therefore, attention sequentially shifts from one to another option, changing the preference for that option. Depending on when a decision is made, different options can be selected. The SEU of each option varies over the course of dynamic situations such that one option during the development of an attack in basketball seems to possess the highest subjective expected utility but seconds later another option may be preferred. Consequently, predictions about which option is chosen are probabilistic in nature, for example, see multi-attribute DFT in Diederich (1995); see also Townsend and Busemeyer (1995) and Johnson (2006) for applications to sport.

In the first step of information processing, DFT follows the extended cumulative SEU in such a way that options are matched subjectively with utilities. Attention and different utilities of the individuals result in different options being preferred. However, the same individual may not always choose the same option in the same situation, even if the subjective expected utilities do not change between the two decisions. Therefore, DFT assumes that if an individual is confronted with the same choice sequentially, that person will randomly assign his or her attention to different options. Because this random process changes attention and individuals choose at different times, DFT explains different choices within and between individuals even when the same situation is encountered again. This is in contrast to utility theories that always predict that the option with the highest subjective utility is chosen. DFT can also describe fluctuations within one decision over time. Samples of preferences are drawn over time until a specific threshold is met, and thresholds are reached by different options at various points in times. Furthermore, samples drawn earlier in the decision-making process will have less impact on the final choice than preference samples drawn just before the decision is made. The field concept in DFT goes back to Lewin (1935) who shows that consequences of actions have a stronger influence on choice just before the choice than in earlier processing states. Consequences can be separated as positive or negative, therefore, some options and their consequences are approached and others are avoided. This also describes why some pairs of options result in longer processing. For instance, it takes longer to decide between two options that a person wants to avoid (e.g., a manager of a financially troubled club deciding between calling the coach to tell him he is fired or calling the bank to ask for more time to make a payment) than between a pair of options composed of one approach and one avoidance option (e.g., firing the coach vs. telling the president of the club about increased sales of team memorabilia).

Finally, DFT defines the time needed to compare pairs of options before the fluctuation of attention drives the system to another pair of options. This also allows for predictions of decision time, a very important feature of fast-paced choices in sport. The prediction of the decision time is built from the sum of comparisons with the simplification that all pairs of comparisons have an equal amount of time. Johnson (2006) provides an example of a football midfield player who needs to make sequential decisions under time pressure in a dynamic situation. These decisions depend on individual preferences such as how much risk a person is prepared to take. Raab and Johnson (2004) showed, for instance, that basketball players have different risk-taking profiles and that these profiles set a specific starting preference for risky or less risky options that allow us to predict fairly accurately the decision time and chosen options of such players. One criticism on the DFT is that it assumes quite a large number of calculations that a person needs to perform. Given the limited time in sport, however, much simpler alternatives have been developed recently.

SIMPLE HEURISTIC APPROACH

A much more radical position compared to the previous theories using some form of utility is taken by the simple heuristics approach developed by Gigerenzer, Todd and the ABC Research Group (1999), which has its origin in the bounded rationality concept by Simon (1956, 1960). Simon argued that as a result of capacity limitations, actual decision makers construct simplified models of complex decision processes – models which contain only the information that the manager perceives that he or she is best able to handle. In fact, bounded rationality (see Simon, 1982, 1987) is a short-hand term suggesting that while individuals may be reasoned and logical, they also have their limits: they interpret and make sense of things within the context of their personal situation while engaging in decision making 'within the box' of a simplified view of a more complex reality. Or as Gigerenzer (2000, p. 125) concisely and elegantly put it: 'How do people make decisions in the real world, where time is short, knowledge lacking, and other resources limited?' This state of affairs makes it difficult to realize the ideal of classical-rational decision making, with the classical-rational model not being able to give an accurate and full description of how most decisions are actually made in real organizations.

As a consequence, bounded rationality implies that only a limited number of decision alternatives and outcomes are considered, which means that managers actually satisfice, rather than strive for, the optimal solutions to problems. Satisficing is defined as choosing the first alternative that appears to give an acceptable or a satisfactory resolution of the problem, or as Simon (cited in Schermerhorn, Hunt and Osborn, 2003, p. 361) stated: 'Most human decision making, whether individual or organizational, is concerned with the discovery and selection of satisfactory alternatives; only in exceptional cases is it concerned with the discovery and selection of optimal decisions.' Simon (1956, 1982) argued that information-processing humans typically needed to satisfice rather than to optimize and maximize. Satisficing, a blend of 'sufficing' and 'satisfying', is a word of Scottish origin, which Simon used to characterize strategies that successfully deal with conditions of limited time, knowledge or computational capacities. His concept of satisficing postulates, for instance, that humans – instead of the intractable sequence of taking the time to survey all possible alternatives, estimating probabilities and utilities for the possible outcomes associated with each alternative, calculating expected utilities, and choosing the alternative that scores highest – would choose the first object that satisfy their aspiration levels, a strategy which would lead to 'good enough' (rather than ideal, maximizing) solutions to the problems at hand.

Within the approach by Gigerenzer, Todd and the ABC Research Group (1999), the concept of utilities is replaced by the concept of simple heuristics. A simple heuristic does not calculate the utilities of options; rather, it is a rule of thumb based on experience that is used to choose between options. One such heuristic is called the recognition heuristic: when choosing between two options, such as which of two cities has a larger population (e.g., San Diego or San Antonio), the option that is recognized is picked (Gigerenzer, Todd and ABC Research Group, 1999). The recognition heuristic predicts that you would choose San Diego if you had never heard of San Antonio, which is, in fact, the correct answer. If you know neither of the options, a random choice is predicted. If you know both options, the recognition heuristic cannot be used and another, more advanced heuristic is enlisted instead. One of these more advanced heuristics is called 'take-the-best'. Consider the city comparison example again and assume you know both cities. The take-the-best heuristic predicts that you would sequentially consider cues that indicate city size, such as whether the city is a state capital or has a famous tourist attraction, in the order of the cues' validity beginning with the highest. If the first cue does not discriminate (here, neither San Diego nor San Antonio is a state capital), you would go to the next cue. If one of the cues is positive for one option but not the other, then take-the-best predicts you choose the city for which the cue is positive and make the decision. For instance, you would choose San Diego because it has a world-famous zoo and you do not know of any similar attraction in San Antonio. Examples of these heuristics are less known in sport but some have been proposed to predict the results of games in football, basketball, and other sport (see Bennis and Pachur, 2006, for an overview).

SUMMARY

Numerous theories have been proposed in decision-making domains that are not specific to sport. Only a limited number of these theories have been applied to sport situations, and these only well after their introduction in psychology, economics and other disciplines. We provide a taxonomy that presents these theories over three dimensions. In the historical overview of these theories we showed that the theories started with rather deterministic and static assumptions such as SEU and became increasingly dynamic and probabilistic as shown in DFT. These theories can explain a number of decision-making problems that exist in sport, however, as exemplified in the theory application box, describe even simple phenomena in a different way. In the following chapters we will provide more specific examples of how these theories can describe and explain some of the phenomena observed in sport.

THEORY APPLICATION

Example: Imagine a playmaker in basketball who needs to decide whether to pass to the centre player or to the left wing player. How would different theories describe this choice process?

Utility theory: Calculate the subjective utilities of the two options (pass to centre, pass to wing) by figuring the product of probability of success and utility value. Choose the option with the highest utility. This theory can describe choices between players that are the result of different subjective utilities as well as different choices of the same individual in different situations that are the result of different assessments of probability of success. It cannot describe different individual choices in the same situation in sequence, how long a decision will take, or the phenomenon of preference reversal.

Take-the-best (simple heuristic): Use the most valid cue first (e.g., base rate of success of centre and wing player), if the base rate is not equal, stop search for further cues and pass to the player with the higher base rate. Take-the-best can explain how people cope with a number of choices and cues under limited time. It can explain preference reversals under time pressure, and how people represent structured information and options. It cannot explain how long a choice will take, and it cannot easily explain how cue validities are learned or how individual differences in the same situation develop.

Decision field theory: Similar to cumulative subjective expected utility theories, calculate utilities for different options, but as attention shifts from one option to another, combinations shift over time until one meets a threshold resulting in a choice. It can explain probability and dynamic choices under time pressure. It can explain differences between and within individuals. It can predict decision time but cannot explain how thresholds are learned or set.

Expertise in JDM

4

Expertise in JDM

What is an expert? For a layperson this seems an easy question, but in expertise research the answer is less straightforward. In the JDM literature in general, the components that distinguish experts from non-experts have not been defined. In sport studies, there is a lack of consensus on what level of training constitutes an expert, such that players with seven years' experience can be labelled novices in one study and experts in another (e.g., Williams *et al.*, 1994). Furthermore, the number of levels of expertise in sport is not standardized. Many experimental studies use two or three levels of expertise arbitrarily to find broad differences between very high and very low expertise. Labels range from naïve, novice or beginner, to expert or master. More abstract coding is also used with descriptions such as low experience, non-experts or high levels of expertise. A recent proficiency scale (see Chi, 2006, adapted from Hoffman, 1998) separates people by ability into naïve (totally ignorant of the domain), novice (minimal exposure to the domain), initiate (a novice who has begun introductory instruction), apprentice (a learner who has received instruction beyond introductory level), journeyman (experienced person with a level of competence), expert (distinguished person who is recognized as such by peers) and master (expert who is perceived by a group of experts as 'the' expert). This general proficiency scale does not specify hours of

Judgement, Decision Making and Success in Sport, First Edition.
M. Bar-Eli, H. Plessner and M. Raab.

experience; however, Ericsson (1996a) provided a rough definition according to which experts in sport have 10 years of experience with 10,000 hours of training. In the remainder of this section we will use the labels expert and novice to differentiate broad levels of expertise, moving to finer scaling in the remaining chapters (for an overview of expertise in sport, see Starkes and Ericsson, 2003).

A definition of decision within the expertise domain is needed as well. According to Yates, 'a decision is a commitment to a course of action that is intended to yield results that are satisfying for specified individuals' (2003, p. 24). Expertise in the JDM domain results in actions that produce good or satisfying consequences (Yates and Tschirhart, 2006), given the definitions of expertise and decisions above. Different levels of expertise are measured by their degree of fast and good decisions. The definition of 'satisfying' or 'good' is not purely based on a desired outcome but is defined in the context of a social environment. For instance, a good decision does not always result in a direct good outcome as a ball allocation may be rated as a better decision than shooting a basketball.

WHAT ARE THE COMPONENTS OF EXPERTISE IN JDM?

Expertise in judgement and decision making is usually broken down into its cognitive components, such as perception, knowledge and decision. In the abovementioned simple heuristics approach, these components are further distilled to a few building blocks such as search, stop and decision rules. In a recent component analysis of expertise and JDM in general, about ten different components were described (Yates and Tschirhart, 2006). In sport, research on JDM expertise primarily follows the general concepts of cognitive psychology, such as those described in the previous chapters on theories of judgement and decision making. We will provide some prototypical examples to illustrate these components in the following chapters of this book.

HOW CAN WE MEASURE JDM EXPERTISE?

The ambiguity of the definition of an expert and the notion of a 'good' choice make it difficult to measure expertise. Therefore, a number of researchers have relied heavily on outcome measures in laboratory-based decision tasks. Recent attempts to measure expertise have used fuller analyses that combine outcome measures of decision quality and decision time with process measures of gaze behaviour or verbal reports (Williams and Ward, 2007). In addition, recent research connects findings in the laboratory with on-court analyses or real competitions (e.g., Ericsson and Williams, 2007). Finally, multitrait, multimethod approaches that concentrate on individual components and typical paradigms have been used to study JDM expertise in sport (Farrow and Raab, 2008). We will focus on three of these components here: perception, knowledge and decision (see Table 4.1).

Perception

JDM expertise can be studied using general perceptual tasks, such as measuring the perceptual visual field, using eye-tracking technology, temporal and spatial occlusion techniques, point-light displays or psychophysiological methods. These methods can be applied to more sport-specific domains by using footage of games in the laboratory or realistic set-ups in the gym. Eye-tracking equipment has become more affordable and portable. Recent research has used this method to capture fixation durations, number of fixations and more complex gaze sequences to describe how visual search behaviour differs among levels of expertise. A main finding is that experts exhibit fewer fixations than novices and that the reduced number of fixations results in better choices (Raab and Johnson, 2007).

The temporal and spatial occlusion paradigm is used to capture expert differences mainly in the anticipation phase of a decision, for instance in basketball, when judging if an opponent will send the ball to the left or right side of the court. Recently two occlusion methods have been combined in a task that uses a video scene of an opponent's

Table 4.1 Cognitive components and paradigms that are used in JDM expertise research (reference indicates a prototypical study).

Component	Paradigm	Pros and Cons
Perception	General perceptual ability tests (Farrow and Raab, 2008)	Pros: general usability Cons: prediction power is limited
	Eye tracking (Williams, Janelle and Davids, 2004)	Pros: general usability Cons: technically extensive; complex dataset and analysis
	Temporal and spatial occlusion techniques (Williams, Davids and Williams, 1999)	Pros: selection of central information Cons: ecological validity is limited
	Point-light (Abernethy *et al.*, 2001)	Pros: extraction of central components Cons: ecological validity is limited
	Psychophysiological methods (Janelle, Duley and Coombes, 2004)	Pros: neurophysiological foundation of concepts Cons: technically extensive; complex dataset and analysis
Knowledge	General knowledge and memory tests (Ericsson and Simon, 1993)	Pros: general use Cons: prediction power is limited
	Recall tests (McPherson and Kernodle, 2003)	Pros: sport- and situation-specific usability Cons: more complex analysis
	Recognition tests (Raab, 2003)	Pros: sport- and situation-specific usability Cons: distinction between perceptual and cognitive recognition limited
	Verbal reports (McPherson, 1999)	Pros: detection of individual problem representation Cons: large database and complex construction of categories
Decision	Option-selection paradigm (Abernethy, 1990)	Pros: sport- and situation-specific usability Cons: technically extensive, complex dataset and analysis
	Option-generation paradigm (Johnson and Raab, 2003)	Pros: reconstruction of decision set and problem representation Cons: complex dataset and ecological validity is limited

movement in badminton. The scene is stopped at different times before or during ball–racket contact and part of the information is occluded, such as when the racket, arm, or head is masked in the video (Hagemann, Strauss and Cañal-Bruland, 2006). In each of the conditions, participants anticipated the position in their own court in which the opponents' smash would end. A main finding is that experts can judge faster and more correctly than novices on participants' performance changes in critical cueing conditions (e.g., Cañal-Bruland, 2009).

Point-light displays reduce the movements of an athlete to a small number of points. Findings suggest that experts are better able than novices at using this reduced information to make choices (Munzert, Hohmann and Hossner, 2010). The mechanisms of such an advantage are currently being explored (e.g., Williams, 2008).

Finally, in recent years combined psychophysical and behavioural methods using EEG and fMRI, among others, have been used to differentiate expertise levels (Janelle, Duley and Coombes, 2004). However, the number of studies in JDM in sport is limited because such methods cannot be used to assess gross movements.

In summary, the perceptual aspect of JDM expertise has been examined by sport-specific methods, albeit in situations of low ecological validity (see Farrow and Raab, 2008). Different aspects of JDM expertise were recently combined in multimethod designs, closing gaps on behavioural and neurophysiological levels.

Knowledge

Knowledge is captured mainly by recognition or recall tests. For instance, a recognition test provides athletes with items that they may or may not have seen before. Experts recognize players' positions in structured game situations faster than novices, whereas there are no differences in unstructured situations (Gobet and Simon, 1996). In recall tests, athletes are asked to recall situations using paper-and-pencil or computer-based tests. Again, experts recall structured situations faster and better than novices. Further evidence indicates that this better recall knowledge is based mainly on experience with these specific situations and is not a general advantage (Allard, Graham and Paarsalu, 1980). A more complex method uses verbal reports during think-aloud procedures or immediately after athletes' decisions in an attempt to capture the thinking process. A main finding here is that the knowledge base is much more advanced in experts compared to novices, but experts also reduce the number of cues and options to the relevant few that represent the problem better (McPherson and Kernodle, 2003).

Knowledge is captured in different ways and it seems appropriate to conclude that the choice of paradigm influences the kind of knowledge the researcher measures. Furthermore, research combining knowledge tests with perception and decision tasks increased over the last years, whereas a systematic integration of these methods is still lacking.

Decision

The decision components are listed here to stress two different paradigms that are worth reporting. The most prominent is the classic option-selection task in which athletes are given a small number of options they have to select between, such as 'will the opponent strike to the left or right?' (Smeeton, Ward and Williams, 2004). An alternative is the option-generation paradigm in which athletes are not presented with a limited and selected set of options but only with the situation (Johnson and Raab, 2003). Participants are instructed to generate an initial intuitive choice, then alternative choices that seem appropriate in this situation, and finally, after building their own choice set, the option they think is the best. The number of options generated, the sequential structure of the generated options as well as the position of the best choice within the generated list of options provide further ways to capture the decision-making process.

HOW CAN WE EXPLAIN JDM EXPERTISE?

We argued that there is ambiguity in the field of expertise concerning the definition of experts, the components of JDM expertise and how to define a 'good' option. Therefore, it is not surprising that there is no unifying theory explaining the relation between different components of JDM and expertise, although the explanations that do exist are much more specific than those promoted decades ago, when talent were used to label differences between distinct levels of expertise. Nowadays, it is generally accepted that specific experience provides the basis for the faster and better choices of experts, which are based on different perceptual, knowledge and decision strategies. We will discuss other explanations for JDM experts and novices in the following chapters.

HOW CAN WE DEVELOP JDM EXPERTISE?

Therese Brisson, Olympic gold medallist of the Canadian ice hockey team in 2002, wrote: 'There is no time in hockey to evaluate all options and pick the best one. You have to choose the first, best one' (Brisson, 2003, p. 216). Experts such as Brisson seem to have a way to judge situations in the blink of an eye. Ericsson, Krampe and Tesch-Römer (1993) considered deliberate practice to be the reason for such extraordinary faculties. According to Ericsson (1996a), the concept of deliberate processes is used if a task is difficult to achieve and feedback, as well as opportunities for repetitive practice and correctional interventions, are available to the trainee. This implies that the amount of practice is less important for a distinction between novices and experts than the quality of practice itself. However, some assumptions of the deliberate practice concept have recently been criticized. For example, interviews revealed that top athletes perceive training experience as non-deliberative, whereas a deliberate approach suggests a more painstaking and unpleasant training (Hodges and Starkes, 1996).

Côté, Baker and Abernethy (2003) brought up an interesting distinction in the development of an expert. They distinguished between 'free play', 'deliberate play', 'organized practice' and 'deliberate practice'. Free play is when the athlete plays without a coach, as one might do for leisure or on a playground. Deliberate play is classified between free play and deliberate practice because the coach brings in situational variations to organize the play. Organized practice is equivalent to the structure of exercise series. Deliberate practice, on the other hand, is defined by its performance-specific, less pleasant training conditions. The authors suggested that the proportion of these four forms of practice shifts in the course of becoming an expert from free and deliberate playing in the beginning of learning to organized and deliberate practice in the later phases of expertise (see also Soberlak and Côté, 2003). However, there are currently no longitudinal studies comparing deliberate practice with the other types of practice defined by Côté, Baker and Abernethy (2003) on the expert level.

Baker, Côté and Abernethy (2003) interviewed a total of 28 players in Canadian national field hockey, netball and basketball teams. The athletes were asked about their practice type and amount of training. On average, the interviewed players had practiced for 13 years with approximately 4,000 training hours before being designated national team players. The participating players were also tagged 'good decision makers' by their coaches. Interestingly, these players had all done various activities not related to their specific sport, including other sports, in their first years of practice. The authors found a negative correlation between the number of non-sport-specific activities and the amount of sport-specific practice before being nominated to the national team. However, to date there have not been any systematic research studies on decision-making differences in experts and novices that could shed light on the effects of sport-specific and non-sport-specific experience on the improvement in decision-making quality and speed.

SUMMARY

The development of expertise is a lengthy process in which athletes choose different routes to excel. Due to the large number of components involved in sport expertise as well as the large array of measurements applied, research in sport expertise has been fairly descriptive and unifying theories are still missing. Explanations of deliberate practice and the description of athletes' development continue to be debated. We will give more specific examples in the following chapters of JDM phenomena observed in sports for athletes, coaches, referees, managers and spectators.

THEORY APPLICATION

Example: How did Tiger Woods, David Beckham and Martina Navratilova become what they are now? The road to excellence is variable, but there are some specific assumptions about how this process can be optimized or accelerated.

Deliberate practice: Ericsson argued that expertise is not a matter of talent but rather of the amount of deliberate practice. Components of that effortful and specialized practice as well as the development of long-term memory for their skills are the basis of the 'expert performance approach' framework.

From play to practice: Côté, Baker and Abernethy (2003) suggested that experts develop through a sequence of play and practice that starts with free and deliberate play and becomes increasingly structured and deliberate practice over years of training. Training factors of play and practice as well as social influences of coaches, peers and family change over the development of expertise.

Athletes

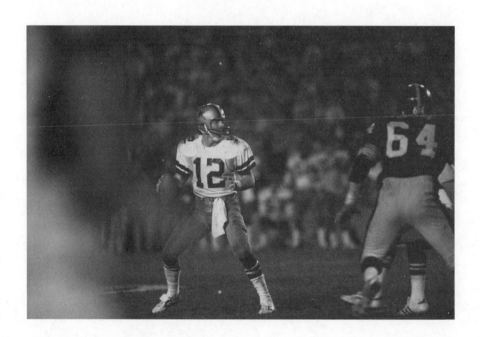

5

Athletes

This chapter starts off by describing how athletes judge their own performance. We suggest that they get their information in a number of ways, through perception and memory as well as with combined strategies integrating internal and external sources of information. Furthermore, we determine which decision-making processes as well as situational and personal variables will lead to a particular utilization of decision-making options and choices by athletes. Finally, we will propose recommendations for a decision-making training and rules of thumb for coaching athletes in the JDM domain.

JUDGING ONE'S OWN PERFORMANCE

Social interactions in sport are highly determined by the way athletes form impressions about each other and how they perceive and evaluate their own performance. For example, in a tennis match, a player may choose her game plan dependent on her impression of her opponent's skills in comparison to her own assets and deficits. If she still looses, it is important for her to know why she did in order to prevent future losses. This brief example already comprises the three main processes that have been addressed in the literature on how athletes judge their own and their opponents' performance: processes of person perception, social comparisons and causal attributions.

Judgement, Decision Making and Success in Sport, First Edition.
M. Bar-Eli, H. Plessner and M. Raab.
© 2011 John Wiley & Sons, Ltd. Published 2011 by John Wiley & Sons, Ltd.

Person perception

People seek actively for information which allows them to form accurate impressions of other people when they engage in social interactions. It can be assumed for athletes that they look out for such information to understand the demands of the (competitive) interaction and to predict how it is likely to progress and conclude (Greenlees, 2007).

As mentioned in Chapter 2, Social cognition, an advantage of categorical thinking is that the application of an adequate category can be a helpful guide in adjusting people's behaviour to the behaviour of their interaction partners (Fiske and Taylor, 2008). Categories, such as a person schema, typically include knowledge that allows inferences beyond the information given in a certain situation. For example, when we play a tennis match against an opponent for the first time, the prior information that the opponent belongs to the category of serve-and-volley players allows us to predict what she will do after her service and to take adequate counter-measures in order to attain our goal of winning the match (e.g., to concentrate on a sharp return). In line with this reasoning, Miki, Tsuchiya and Nishino (1993) found participants in a simulated golf contest to be influenced by prior information about the alleged strength of their opponent. Thus, just as in normal life, people seek actively for information that allows them to form accurate impressions of other people when they engage in social interactions. It can be assumed for competitions in sport that athletes look for cues that facilitate appropriate categorization of their opponents. Therefore, it is surprising that the impression-formation process among athletes has received little attention in the corresponding literature so far. In two studies, however, Greenlees and colleagues examined the influence of an opponent's body language and clothing on the first impressions formed by observers in tennis (Greenlees, Buscombe et al., 2005) and in table tennis (Greenlees, Bradley et al., 2005). Body language and clothing were chosen as variables because other researchers have suggested that they are important interpersonal cues. While the influence of clothing is not obvious in both studies, there is strong evidence that body language exerts an influence on the impression-formation process of athletes even when playing performance is viewed. Players that displayed positive body language (e.g., erect posture) were rated, for example, as more assertive, competitive, experienced, confident and fitter than players displaying negative body language (e.g., hunched posture). In addition, participants reported higher expectations of success against tennis players displaying negative body language than against tennis players displaying positive body language (Greenlees, Buscombe *et al.*, 2005). Accordingly, the authors argue that the development of performance expectancies in the observation of a player's body language in the warm-up can directly affect his opponent's performance. Although it is evident from these studies that body language influences impression formation among athletes beyond the directly observed performances, this does not necessarily lead to wrong assessments of an opponent's strength. After all, a positive body language can indeed be an indicator of a self-confident, good tennis player. However, the knowledge of the influence of these cues on an opponent's impression can also cause an athlete to use them in a strategic or even deceptive way (Gilbert and Jamison, 1994; Hackfort and Schlattmann, 2002). Thus, a promising direction for future research would be to study the validity of the different categorical cues that athletes use in competitions to form accurate impressions of their opponents.

Social comparison

A priority source of information in order to judge the self is the comparison with other people (Festinger, 1954; Mussweiler, 2003). The judgement of an athlete's performance is frequently based on the comparison with other athletes, or with prior judgements of other athletes' performance. Accordingly, several studies show that social comparisons determine evaluative processes in judging athletes in various sports. For example, Ebbeck (1990) examined the sources of information used by exercisers to judge performance, who were enrolled in a university weight-training programme. They had to evaluate the importance of various information sources in judging weight-training performance, for example, instructor feedback, student comparison and performance in workout. It was found, especially for males, that they predominantly relied on social comparison variables and consequently were more likely to process information relative to others.

Gotwals and Wayment (2002) assessed the usefulness of 10 types of evaluative information of an athlete's perception for evaluating their athletic performance, examined whether these self-evaluative strategies were associated with self-esteem and examined the impact of these strategies on athletic performance. They found that personal standards were rated as the most useful form of information with downward social comparisons and feared selves information as the least useful. Athletes high in self-esteem used more personal standards and ideal selves information and fewer feared selves. Higher self-esteem was associated with better athletic performance. However, the comparison standard may also vary depending on the skill level of athletes. In a corresponding study on the self-evaluation of tennis players, Sheldon (2003) could show that beginners were more likely to value temporal comparisons and advanced players were more likely to value social comparisons. Players rating tennis as highly important were more likely to value temporal comparisons and effort for self-assessment. In a study with professional football players, Van Yperen (1992) found that the self-enhancement through social comparisons does also depend on the importance of the judged dimension and ambiguity of the comparison standard.

Causal attributions

Once a certain outcome of a sport event has been assessed, either objectively or subjectively, athletes automatically tend to ask why this outcome has happened. Attributions are answers to this question and, thus, the product of a causal analysis in which the goal is to identify the factors that led to a certain outcome (see Chapter 2, Social cognition). People are most likely to make attributions when they are confronted with unexpected, important or negative events. When people come up with an attribution for a certain event, this will influence their subsequent thoughts, feelings and, most importantly, their behaviour. Attributions play an important part in the domain of sport. For example, following failure in a competition, athletes have to identify the reasons for this to be able to adapt the following training sessions accordingly (for more detailed overviews see, e.g., Biddle, Hanrahan and Sellars, 2001; Rees, Ingledew and Hardy, 2005).

Most of the research on attributions in the field of sport focuses on the influence of the outcome of an event – that is, perceived success and failure – on subsequent attributions. These studies investigated whether athletes, as well as fans and the media, display a self-serving bias, that is, a tendency to take credit for success and deny responsibility for failure (Fiske and Taylor, 2008). An attribution may be called self-serving, if one benefits from it by means of maintaining or enhancing one's self-esteem. Thus, attributing failure to an external and unstable cause (e.g., the weather) may have a self-protecting effect – likewise, attributing success to an internal and stable cause (e.g., ability) may have a self-enhancing effect.

Mullen and Riordan (1988) conducted a meta-analysis on the self-serving bias in sports. The authors found evidence for a self-serving bias on the locus of causality (internal vs. external) dimension. People make more internal attributions (e.g., to achievement, effort) following success than following failure. The authors also found that this effect increased with team size, meaning the effect was larger for attributions to the team in team sports than to the individual in individual sports. They concluded from this finding that the self-serving bias may be better explained by cognitive (information processing) than motivational factors.

However, studies by Sherman and Kim (2005) underline the importance of motivational factors for the self-serving bias. In their studies, they provide evidence for a self-protective function of the self-serving as well as the group-serving bias. In general, participants made more internal attributions as well as attributions to their team after experiencing victory than defeat. This tendency was eliminated for participants who completed an affirmation of personal values beforehand.

A study by Fiedler and Gebauer (1986) offers the perceptual perspective of athletes as an additional factor to explain the self-serving bias. They found strong evidence of a self-serving as well as a group-serving bias for football players. However, this bias was stronger for defenders than for midfielders and strikers. The authors explain this with the different perceptual perspectives of the players due to their position in the team. When a team is winning, defenders of that team will focus more on their own players; when a team is losing, defenders of that team will focus more on the players of the other team. The perspective for midfielders and strikers of winning compared to losing teams is more balanced. Thus, the self-serving bias may be caused by motivational as well as cognitive and perceptual factors.

Another well-known attributional bias is the self-centred bias. The self-centred bias is the tendency to take more than one's share of responsibility for a jointly produced outcome (Fiske and Taylor, 2008) and it seems to be most relevant for team sports. It can be seen as the stronger tendency for self-serving relative to group-serving attributions. Brawley (1984) found evidence for a self-centred attributional style for dyads of doubles tennis players as well as for dyads of coaches and athletes regarding their responsibility attributions.

Taken together, the work on biases in attributions of sport performance suggests that self-serving tendencies may be seen as the dominant principle underlying these biases.

Apart from the general attributional biases outlined above, there are also individual attributional styles or biases. One important attributional style relevant to the field of sport is the pessimistic explanatory style that may lead to learned helplessness (e.g., Martin-Krumm et al., 2003). Learned helplessness is the belief that one has no control over negative events such as failure during a competition. Attributing negative events to internal, stable and global causes is called a pessimistic explanatory style. Seligman et al. (1990) demonstrated the negative consequences of such a pessimistic explanatory style. In a study using members of two college swimming teams as participants, they demonstrated that pessimistic swimmers showed more unexpected poor performances during competition than optimistic swimmers. They also demonstrated that performance of pessimistic swimmers deteriorated after receiving (false) negative feedback, whereas this feedback did not affect performance of optimistic swimmers.

This example shows that biased attributions may have negative consequences for future performances and the success of athletes during competitions. If attributions have these consequences, one should try to exchange them with more positive attributions. Interventions with this goal are called 'attributional retraining'. The dimensions of stability and controllability have been the focus for most of attributional retraining studies in the field of sport. For example, Orbach, Singer and Murphey (1997) manipulated the attributional style of college basketball players. Players were instructed either to make attributions to controllable, unstable factors (e.g., effort, strategy) or to uncontrollable, stable factors (e.g., ability). Players in a control group received no instructions. The results showed that it was possible to modify attributions and performance regarding a basketball performance task. Participants making attributions to controllable, unstable factors outperformed participants in the other two groups in a dribbling task. Taken together, these studies show that attributional retraining is possible and has positive effects on future performance.

WHAT CHOICES ARE ATHLETES CONFRONTED WITH?

'Reading defences, reading coverages, how to study, how to prepare', were the most important things his coaches taught him. This is what the American football legend Joe Montana said in a speech in honour of his enshrinement in the Pro Football Hall of Fame (http://www.profootballhof.com/story/2000/7/29/753/).

We will focus predominantly on those areas in which short-term decisions during practice and competition are relevant. Questions include how athletes pick up environmental information, how this information is extracted from memory to form decisions (perception and memory), how much information and what particular pieces of information are used and in which order these bits of information are applied (visual search strategies, attention and concentration).

Consider the situation of a quarterback when he goes back into the game, there will be 21 more players to be perceived on the 110 × 70-yard football field. His real-time perception of continuously changing conditions on the field will be complemented by information from his memory comprising previous behaviours in specific situations and his coach's last time-out instructions. We will depict the perceptual and memory processes that enable the quarterback to meet the corresponding requirements and conditions in perception and memory.

Perception

For many years, scientific research on perception in the field of decision making in sport has concentrated on the visual system almost to the exclusion of all else. Only with the desire for further improvements in sports requiring senses other than vision has research on auditory and tactile information and balance performance gained prominence (Williams and Ward, 2003). For instance, questions such as how structured auditory information can increase the learning speed of a movement in swimming have only recently been analysed in experiments (Effenberg, 2005; Gray, 2008). The connection between different sensory information settings has been investigated in a couple of studies (see Anderson, Snyder, Bradley and Xing, 1997).

The fact that it is basic sensory skills that allow for decision-making processes seems to be beyond dispute. For example, the size of the visual field (part of the visual environment that can be perceived during eye fixation) influences decision-making performance of handball players (Farrow and Raab, 2008). While the size of the visual field cannot be enlarged, the effective use of the entire visual field can be practiced to some extent (see Williams and Ward, 2003). Therefore, differences in the size of the visual field of athletes and non-athletes can rather be ascribed to selection bias and limited functional use of the visual field. Apart from the visual field, there are a few visual parameters that cannot be practiced (see Abernethy, 1990, for an overview). This is why these parameters are relevant for analysing and defining base rates in talent scouting.

There is one important parameter for peripheral vision in the field of sensual perception: perception beyond the viewer's actual focus (see Savelsbergh *et al.*, 2005). Studies in this field show that athletes possess the ability of 'synchro-optical' perception, which means they are able to perceive visual information that is parallel in time and they can separate spatial components of these perceptions. Furthermore, if multimodal information can be integrated, studies show that synchro-optical perception can be learned (Effenberg, 2005; Gray, 2008). Performance of different sensory systems influences decision making in the early stages of information processing, resulting in consequences at later levels of information processing (Gray, 2008). In summary, a number of sensory systems influence the decisions, but that does not mean that training them in isolation has beneficial effects on decision making. For instance, visual training hardly improves decision making in sports, since movement information has to be processed actively (Abernethy and Wood, 2001; Farrow and Raab, 2008).

Memory

Apart from different bits of environmental information, athletes' decisions are also influenced by information from memory. Here, experts distinguish between the type of information, for example, factual vs. procedural knowledge, and the duration of representation, for example, short-term vs. long-term memory (Magill, 2007). A mutual finding in studies on different sports shows that knowledge used in decision making is rather sport-specific and contextual. An overview on the distinction of experts and novices by Williams and Ward (2003) points out that experts exhibit better performance in recalling tasks only under sport-specific structures and environments. In addition, Williams and Ward showed in a cross-sectional study with 9- to 17-year-old football players that situational probabilities for specific alternative actions in experts are more effectively represented in memory. The accuracy of anticipating actions of players and the evaluation of important excellent scorers in unique situations improves over age. Differences between skilled and unskilled players regarding the above variables can be found in children as young as nine years old. Summing up, memory processes are well known to interact with current perceptions to influence decisions. However, it has not yet been researched to a great extent on how long-term and short-term memory are dynamically involved in such choices.

Visual search strategies

In sport, situations can change in the blink of an eye. Yet, a quarterback has to evaluate his planned decisions according to the ever-changing situational context. Whether he opts to throw a pass to his teammate or to press forward a few more yards also depends on the order in which information is processed. This means, it is not enough to know merely what kind of information, from memory or the environment, a player uses but how this information is used. For instance, research in the field of visual search strategies showed that the information processed during decision-making phases varies dramatically between and within players of different levels of expertise (Raab and Johnson, 2007).

Visual search strategies describe what kind of and how much information is gathered at a particular point in time and when the search for information will be stopped to make a decision. For example, consider again a playmaker in football who has to scan during his movements the changes of team players and the defence to decide within a fraction of a second where to pass the ball. Search strategies have been analysed in various sports using different tasks and performance levels. The corresponding research methods can be categorized into four different areas: eye tracking, occlusion, interview and point-light displays. All of these methods are used to describe search strategies and build a better understanding of how decisions are influenced by these strategies or how to improve visual training programmes.

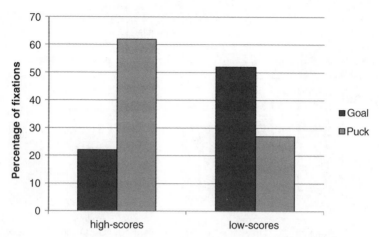

Figure 5.1 The percentage of fixations of high scoring ice-hockey players in comparison to low scoring players shortly before the execution of a penalty shot (Martell and Vickers, 2004).

Eye tracking. Eye tracking is used to measure eye movements while an athlete is viewing a picture or video clip. Gaze can also be tracked during realistic field situations such as ice hockey using the recognition-primed model of Klein (1989) introduced earlier (Martell and Vickers, 2004). Just before the final execution of a penalty shot the percentage of fixations of high scoring players was much more toward the puck, whereas the low scoring shooters fixates an area of the goal (see Figure 5.1). Under simple task structures the athletes, for example in rugby, have to decide if an attack should be executed or not (Jackson, Warren and Abernethy, 2006). Under more complex task structures, the athletes are also asked to give tactical evaluations in a specific situation, such as where the ball should be played next in a particular attacking situation in football (Williams, Davids and Williams, 1999, for an overview). Currently, this research method can investigate differences in the number, type and order of pieces of information between different groups of expertise.

Occlusion. The technique of occlusion is applied to mask certain aspects of a picture or a video. Studies in squash (Abernethy, 1990) and football (Williams and Davids, 1998) showed to what extent the efficiency of decision making deteriorated under spatial occlusion

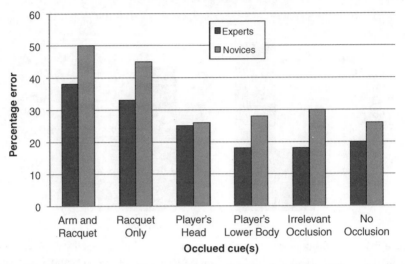

Figure 5.2   Percentage error in the prediction of stroke direction by different occlusion conditions for experts and novices in squash (Abernethy, 1990).

(occlusion of certain parts of a movement) or temporal occlusion (reduced temporal information of a movement). For instance, errors from experts were most reduced compared to errors from novices when arm and racquet were spatially occluded (see Figure 5.2). In addition, the percentage error difference between experts and novices was highest two frames before ball–racquet contact using temporal occlusion (Abernethy, 1990).

Furthermore, Williams and Davids found differences in search strategies between experienced and less experienced football players in one-on-one attacking situations but not in three-on-one situations. Experienced players fixate more information with a shorter duration and they fixate the hip area of the opponent longer than less experienced football players. In another study, Ripoll (1988) demonstrated that gaze strategies are functionally different according to the function of their users (coaches, playmaker, attacker). This could implicitly provide evidence for the significance of this information for decision making.

Interview. Interviews can help researchers collect and analyse verbalizable knowledge within decision making from a more subjective view. Since it is quite difficult to gather verbal information from a moving athlete, mainly retrospective interviewing techniques are used in sports. In tennis, for example, researchers have used time-outs or the aftermath of the game to conduct their interviews. McPherson and Kernodle (2003) found that the relation between verbalizable knowledge and tactical performance does not have to correlate compellingly in a positive manner. Some beginners, for example, may occasionally name a lot more options than experienced tennis players, but beginners obviously do not play on the same level as experts because the options generated from the experts fit well to the situation at hand.

Point-light displays. Point-light displays present points of light on joints, viewed in darkness which reduce the total on-screen movement of an athlete to a certain number of dots of light. They can represent either all or part of a movement (Johansson, 1973). Abernethy and Parker (1989) showed in a squash study that the presentation of a squash movement by just 26 point-lights was sufficient to have the participant anticipate the correct hitting direction and speed without any significant adverse effects in comparison to a video presentation of the same movement.

This list of methods should not lead to the false conclusion that researchers are interested in the methods per se. They rather apply combined research paradigms such as eye tracking and interviews to discover the mechanisms of expertise difference in many sports. One approach, using multimethods, showed that there is a 70% consistency between verbal reports and eye movements with female gymnasts who had to view a video of a gymnastic programme (see Vickers, 1988). Most of these methods are used also in training programmes. However, reviews indicate that the acquisition of visual search strategies has received little attention to date (but see Jackson and Farrow, 2005).

Attention and concentration

What does the quarterback do in his next move, given so many options available and information changing in fractions of a second? Attention to specific players in football and concentration are crucial competences. Therefore, athletes need to know how many opponents and team players and how many options to choose from are sufficient. Sometimes just concentrating on one single team player to detect the right moment to make a pass is sufficient. Attention, also known as selective perception and the concept of concentration, which implies focusing on particular information, are significant parameters that affect decision making of athletes. In particular, the information focused on in the state of attention does influence the choice from a given set of available options. Attention significantly influences choices in different situations and tasks (Williams and Ward, 2007). Generally, attention is classified as focused or divided. A basketball player, for example, has to perform both: divided attention during an attack, when he is observing many team players at the same time; and focused attention, when he fixates the basketball hoop before taking the shot. But in team sports, players divide attention more often than athletes in individual sports.

Selectivity of information is another quite important dimension that differs individually, task specifically and situationally. That is, experts are more apt than novices to direct their attention to task-specific information. In this context, some authors have also pointed out individual differences (Singer *et al.*, 1991). For instance, it is found that task-irrelevant cognition is more prevalent in situation-oriented persons (reserved behaviour) than in action-oriented persons (dynamic behaviour).

In summary, the previous methods used to detect visual search patterns need to be brought together to the aforementioned conceptions of attention and concentration in much more detail than previously investigated to provide a cornerstone on how athletes choose.

HOW DO ATHLETES CHOOSE?

An experienced quarterback has gone through hard training during his career, so he is pretty good at perception and selection of information using attention and concentration. In addition to this, he has had to learn in which order information should be gathered. The strategies taught to him will determine how his tactical knowledge is used. How does he now decide which options he will take into consideration and which he will eventually choose?

Decision-making processes can be displayed in different phases during the execution of tactical decisions. Using a two-factor model, Bunker and Thorpe (1982) distinguished 'what-decisions' (what kind of action is to be performed) and 'how-decisions' (how this action is to be performed). In the field of motor programme theories (e.g., Schmidt, 1975), this classification corresponds to the difference between programming decisions (e.g., throw or pass in handball) and parameter decisions (e.g., throw to the lower left or right of the goal). Decision-making processes within this two-factor model comply with Heckhausen's (1989) theory of action. It says that the option with the highest result of valence multiplied by probability of success will be chosen. Alternatively, there are process models that describe separate components of decision-making processes. These models are designed to explain how options are generated and which options are eventually taken under a particular time constraint and according to available (self-generated or given) options. Some process models do not assume that the choice of options is subject to a calculation of valence and probability of success; rather, only a few options are taken into account and only a small amount of information is sufficient to choose between options based on expertise (Johnson and Raab, 2003). A consequence of these different models is that a number of conflicting practical considerations, which need further empirical testing, can be build.

Option generation

Option generation refers to the process that there is no pre-set of alternatives in any dynamic situation in which an athlete has to generate options. The aforementioned quarterback, for instance, has to decide which action he will choose from an extensive pool of options. Findings in the field of chess showed that highly skilled chess players consider fewer options than medium-skilled players, though, or in particular, because highly skilled players possess more experience in and knowledge of judging specific chess situations (Klein *et al.*, 1995). Even more important for the process of generating options is the fact that, when making their final choice, good chess players frequently prefer the first chess move they generated during the decision-making process (Klein *et al.*, 1995). In his recognition-primed model, Klein (2003) described such option generation as a two-part process. First, in a kind of pattern recognition, a chess player compares current chess situations with experience associated with solutions to similar situations in the past. Second, the chess player executes a mental simulation of consequences for the recalled solutions applied to the current situation. If the evaluation outcome is positive, the chess player may take the first adequate option to solve the current situation. This phenomenon has also been demonstrated in critical areas of decision making, such as the decisions of fire fighters or military personnel (see Klein, 2003, for an overview).

   In tennis, contrary to predictions of McPherson and Kernodle (2003), novices generated more options than experienced tennis players although novices at the same time verbalized less tactical knowledge. Johnson and Raab (2003) analysed the process of option generation in handball. In their study, about 80 handball players of different ages and performance levels viewed tactical situations presented on video. The video sequences were picked beforehand by handball experts according to how they match realistic situations in a game, availability of options in these situations and the number of adequate options. The video was stopped when a specific player possessed the ball. The participant then had to name the first option that came to his or her mind, name further appropriate options for the current situation and finally choose the best option. Research results reaffirmed the take-the-first heuristic, which assumes that the first option generated is better than any other option generated subsequently (see Figure 5.3). Additionally, it was proven that the quality of all subsequent options decreased linearly according to their conformity to the presented situation (validity of options). Finally, the results showed that experts stop the process of option generation after generating just a few options and then pick the first or one of the first options generated. Less skilful players, however, generated more options and in most cases did not pick any of the first

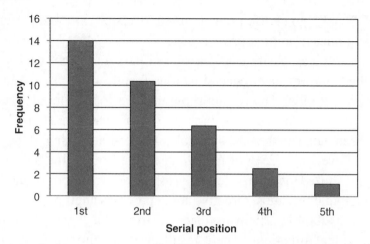

Figure 5.3 Frequency of 'appropriate' option generation in handball, as rated by experts, summed over participants and trials, for the generated options in each serial position (Johnson and Raab, 2003).

options generated. So far, it has not been clarified how experts learn such reduction of options during the process of option generation.

Option selection

Experimental studies have completely dispensed with option-generation processes (see the preceding section for exceptions) and, instead, they have confronted athletes with a pre-set of given options. In sport, there are already a huge number of studies dealing with option selection (see Williams and Ward, 2003, for an overview). Similar to the research designs for studies on visual search strategies described above, research on option choice has applied several different methods of analysis. At the formal process level, however, valid models only describe the range of option choices (see Raab, 2002, for an overview). Apart from the two-factor model of tactical decisions based on Heckhausen's (1989) action theory, there are only a few simulations that include tactical decision-making processes (see Alain and Sarrazin, 1990; Raab, 2002).

Currently, the most comprehensive implementation of task, situation and personality variables within decision-making processes in sports has been accomplished with decision field theory as described above (Busemeyer and Townsend, 1993). Due to its dynamic parameters, the DFT is able to clarify predictions for decision time and preference reversal under time pressure.

In this context, Raab (2002) analysed pass and shoot decisions of basketball players in offence situations (centre rotation) via tactical video presentation. The results show that the four different pass and shoot options (take the shot, pass to a teammate: point guard, post, centre) depended on the time available for decision making. If there was less time available (25% of the average time for making a decision), decisions shifted toward a safe option (pass back to the point guard) and the option that was most effective at the previous attempt. If the whole time was available, participants made decisions that were appropriate to the individual situations. These results were confirmed by means of computer simulations with a DFT parameter for decisions under time pressure of 25% and 50% of the usually available time. This parameter (z parameter) displays an anchor point for the preference of deciding between two alternatives. The initial preference for one or another option during a series of decisions could depend on how successful a decision maker was with the last decision made or when and how often an option was taken into consideration in the past.

An athlete exposed to high time pressure will have more difficulty considering current environmental information and so the option with the highest initial preference is likely to be chosen. When time is abundant, this will compensate for the initial preference and will shift preference to an option other than the one that was initially preferred (preference reversal).

The initial preference can also be influenced by personality factors. In a video-based study, Raab and Johnson (2004) found that in on-screen decision-making situations, action-oriented athletes (vs. state orientation) dared to take more shots than their less action-oriented counterparts (Kuhl and Beckmann, 1994). Yet, results also showed that this phenomenon could be explained by higher initial preference for risky options within action-oriented athletes and higher initial preference for low-risk options within state-oriented athletes.

A recent trend within individual choices of athletes refers to football. For example, from the perspective of the shooter, Masters, van der

Kamp and Jackson (2007) showed that in penalty situations athletes tend to shoot more to the left when the goalkeeper is slightly positioned to the right and vice versa.

Bar-Eli *et al.* (2007) analysed 286 penalty kicks in top football leagues and championships worldwide and revealed that, given the probability distribution of kick direction, the optimal strategy for goalkeepers is to stay in the goal's centre: goalkeepers, however, almost always jump right or left (see Figure 5.4). Bar-Eli *et al.* (2007) proposed the following explanation for this behaviour: because the norm is to jump, norm theory (Kahneman and Miller, 1986) implies that a goal scored yields more negative feelings for the goalkeeper following inaction (staying in the centre) than following action (jumping), leading to a bias for action. The omission bias, a bias in favour of inaction (see Ritov and Baron, 1990, 1992, 1995) is reversed here because the norm in this case is reversed – to act rather than to choose inaction. The claim that jumping is the norm is supported by a second study: a survey conducted with 32 top professional goalkeepers. The seemingly biased decision making is particularly striking since the goalkeepers have huge incentives to make correct decisions and it is a decision they encounter frequently (see also Azar and Bar-Eli, 2008).

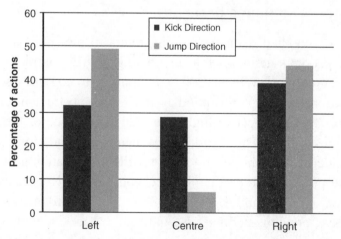

Figure 5.4   The (independent) probability distribution of goalkeepers' jump direction and kickers' scoring direction during penalties in football (Bar-Eli *et al.*, 2007).

Bar-Eli and Azar (2009) argued that, although the outcome of penalty kicks in football might be of utmost importance, shooting strategy is often based more on intuition than on careful research. To determine, what the kicker's best strategy should be, data on 311 penalty kicks in top leagues and championships worldwide were analysed. The results suggested that kicks to the upper area of the goal are the most difficult to stop. A survey of top goalkeepers revealed that they were most satisfied when they stopped a high kick – especially to the top corners and missing such a kick caused the least dissatisfaction. Based on these findings, Bar-Eli and Azar (2009) suggested that the best shooting strategy of penalty kicks may be to aim to the upper two corners and that proper training should help reduce the rate of missing such kicks. In other words, when the kicker shoots to one of the upper corners, his or her situation is similar to that of a basketball player who shoots a foul: the outcome depends mainly on him- or herself, with the behaviour of the goalkeeper being basically irrelevant. However, when the kick is shot to another area of the goal (i.e., not to one of the upper corners), then the goalkeeper's behaviour can be optimized through proper coaching, as suggested by Bar-Eli *et al.* (2007; see also Azar and Bar-Eli, 2008).

Movements influence decision

The term embodied decision making refers to the processes which underlie people's actions while interacting with a complex and dynamic environment (Wilson, 2002). In contrast to cognitive sciences, the traditional view of the mind is that of an abstract information processor. This perspective highlights the significance of the mind's connections to the outside world. Thus, perceptual and motor systems are considered to be highly relevant for the understanding of central cognitive processes, for example, decision making (for an overview see Raab, Johnson and Heekeren, 2009). In accordance with this perspective, previous findings also indicate that task-specific changes (e.g., approach or avoidance) in a movement influence the type of decision-making process, whereas research has mainly accentuated the influence of cognition on motion (Raab and Green, 2005). The preference for forehand strokes in tennis, for example, may present this side to the opponent more frequently. Cause-and-effect of cognition and motion can also be considered the other way round though. For instance, communicative motor skills and movements applied in different behavioural therapies have proven to help influence cognitive processes positively. In this context, the influence of exercise, such as running, on depression has already been exhaustively investigated (see Ernst *et al.*, 2006).

Is it then also plausible that movements – due to their specific positions or functions – can make people think in a more creative or positive way and trigger more heuristic-style information processing? William James (1884) came up with such ideas more than a century ago, when he formulated his hedonic hypothesis stating that flectional and extensional contractions of effectors are correlated with pleasant and unpleasant emotions. James's thesis was extended by the assumption that particular movements influence cognitive processing. Cacioppo, Priester and Berntson (1993) showed that somatic activities resulting from arm extensions and flexions cause different effects on the opinion and evaluation of a cognitive task. Later Friedman and Förster (2000) found that participants could solve creative cognitive tasks better when they pressed one arm in a flexed position against the table as opposed to pressing the arm in an extended position on the table. The authors explained these phenomena by an activation of heuristic or creative processes through flexion of the arm and an activation of systematic processes through extension of the arm. That is, in evolution, the extension of limbs has always been associated with negative experience (avoidance) whereas flexion has always been related to positive experience (approach). Therefore, cognitive structures are enabled to activate creative processes in conditions of approach motivation.

Raab and Green (2005) investigated a functional explanation for the above effect. The corresponding model MOVID (MOVements Influence Decisions), which describes the influence of motion on cognition, assumes that the function of a specific movement influences systematic or heuristic cognition within decision-making processes. Accordingly, it was hypothesized that starting from a steadily flexed elbow in a 90-degree position, heuristic information processing would only occur with a pulling movement, whereas systematic information processing would only be expected with a pushing movement. The same effects are assumed with initial extension and a starting elbow angle of zero degrees. Results indicate that movements do influence cognitive information processing. However, unlike Friedman and Förster's (2000) explanation, the current findings suggest that it is not the mere position of the arm but the function of the movement that is responsible here.

Coping strategies

Consider the following situation: seconds before the end of a football game the score is tied. During the last time-out the coach gives the quarterback important final information. The quarterback now has to cope with the pressure of the crucial, final seconds in the game. What strategies did he learn and how will he cope with the upcoming challenge? Coping strategies are either problem-focused or emotion-focused measures to master a specific situation (see Weinberg and Gould, 2007) and can include task focusing, mind control, self-talk and time management, among other strategies. Decisions under time pressure in competitive situations, as described above, have to be managed by applying coping strategies (see Anshel, Williams and Hodge, 1997; Bar-Eli and Tenenbaum, 1989a, 1989b). Coping strategies have been proven to be a predictor for competitive performance. In a baseball study, Smith and Christensen's (1995) predictions of players' performance in competition and their continuance in professional baseball, using the coping skills inventory ACSI-28, were more reliable than predictions by baseball experts or last-season scoring statistics. Subsequent results also indicated that intervention in coping with stressful situations in sports can be generalized to other areas of life (G. Smith, 1999).

Long-term decisions

A number of long-term decisions are often considered as research questions from a judgement and decision-making perspective in sport. We will focus on doping and career decisions; two choices that are not well researched but are important and bear the potential to inform people making such choices with big consequences. Athletes considering these choices often have very simple questions such as 'Should I dope' or 'Should I end my career'. Answers how they build a choice and evaluate the consequences of these decisions are not well understood yet.

To dope or not to dope

Doping in sport is traced back to ancient Greece and as old as around 3000 years (Emmanouel, 1947). Within this century, doping among athletes gained more scientific attention than ever before, however, often with a rather pessimistic demonstration that the current strategies to stop drug abuse are not sufficient.

For instance, it is stated that the current drug tests and association policies providing negative lists are ineffective (Bird and Wagner, 1997) and rather costly (Yesalis and Cowart, 1998). Alternatives ranging from re-analysing the reasons for or against drug use for adult athletes (Kious, 2008), establishing a collegial enforcement system (Bird and Wagner, 1997) or increasing health education prevention (Laure and Lecerf, 2002) are still rather untested. Another critique at the current practice refers to methods used to elicit drug use, either by expensive laboratory tests (e.g., approximately US $120 per test; Yesalis and Cowart, 1998) or self-reports which provide an underestimation of the prevalence rates of drug users. Simon et al. (2006) used a randomized response technique (RRT) to reduce response errors. The RRT provides a more unbiased response of athletes, because the response is either predetermined by the system or reflects a direct answer of the athlete unknown to the experimenter. Results showed that using RTT increases responses dramatically toward drug use (Simon et al., 2006).

A further line of research reveals that the motives of drug use span the physical, psychological and social aspects of sport performance. For example, US athletes frequently self-report motives of performance enhancement such as reducing pain, increasing energy and becoming competitive, followed by psychological motives such as reducing anxiety and fear of failure or increasing self-confidence (Anshel, 1991). In recent years, the number of national surveys on such causes of drug use in sport increased and has been differentiated to specific subgroups by gender, expertise and sport type. The research is still lacking a theoretical account on if or if not a person will choose to use drugs.

For a book on judgement and decision making in sports, the information about how people decide or judge drug use is far from being satisfactory. In most papers, a natural way to describe the doping problem was in a cost–benefit analysis but without analysing the 'costs' and 'benefits' in a precise qualitative or quantitative way. It is known that most parents judge drug use in sports negatively. Still it does not influence them to allow their children to participate in high doping sports (Nocelli *et al.*, 1998). What cues are considered prior to such judgements are still not known. Furthermore, informed decision-making models of drug use in sport exist but they are quite ambiguous about how to derive the decision. For instance, Bouchard, Weber and Geiger (2002) presented a seven-stage informed decision model for using amphetamines, over-the-counter sympathomimetics and caffeine, which consists of seven questions:

1 Is it 'fair' to take the substance or has its use been banned or restricted?
2 Is the substance legal to purchase, possess and use with regard to civil or common laws?
3 Is taking the substance performance enhancing or performance degrading?
4 Are there health benefits associated with taking the substance and, if so, by what mechanisms?
5 Does this substance cause medical side effects?

6 Are there safety considerations for the user and/or for those near the user?

7 What are the financial implications of substance use? (Bouchard, Weber and Geiger, 2002, p. 209)

How do athletes use such questions and what is the prescription to use such a list of questions? Whether people should not use a specific drug if they think drug use is fair and how they should add and weigh the positive and negative answers for a cost–benefit analysis is not yet analysed.

To stop the career or not to stop it

The decision to end one's career seems to be one of the most important decisions for athletes, as they are, with some exceptions, a termination. Therefore, the transition to end the career is the most popular studied transition in sports on which we will focus (Wylleman, Alfermann and Lavallee, 2004). Within the transition phase, the pre-retirement planning phase seems to play the most important role on whether the transition will gain positive outcomes (Pearson and Petipas, 1990). Thus, it seems natural that many of the national career transition programmes include decision making besides many other personal and social skills (Wylleman, Alfermann and Lavallee, 2004, for a list of national intervention programmes). Still, the level of decision-making strategy often is limited to a description of advantages and disadvantages of retirement and factors that influence the quality of the sport career termination process.

For instance, Erpic, Wylleman and Zupancic (2004) differentiate between athletic and non-athletic factors (see Würth, Lee and Alfermann, 2004, for social factors). Within non-athletic factors positives ones are graduation, birth of a child and a new job. Negative factors are death of family members, friends, injuries and loss of a job. Within the athletic factors, psychological, psychosocial and occupational difficulties are listed as well as the organization of post-sport life. Results indicate that most important for high quality career transitions is whether the career was stopped voluntarily and if all sport achievements have been fulfilled. But which factors are used in which manner in a decision process was not yet described in transition research in sports.

An exception is the work of Petlichkoff (1988). It analysed the satisfaction of different groups of athletes during a season. It was predicted and shown that the cost–benefits measures of satisfaction are highest for starters and lowest for dropouts. The theoretical explanation was given by the social exchange theory (Thibaut and Kelley, 1959, applied to sports by Smith, 1986), which describes an individual's motivation via maximizing rewards and minimizing costs. Importantly, the subjective weightings of benefits and costs relative to his or her standards of satisfaction are implemented in the cost–benefit measure and a description of a point when an individual's sport participation can change from satisfying to unsatisfying. Beyond this early work of modelling the decision process itself, little is known of how athletes choose to end their career.

JDM TRAINING FOR ATHLETES

What does the quarterback's practice look like when he possesses all the decision-making competences described above? To what extent is practice sport-specific? How independent of specific decision-making competences should practice be? Decision-making processes are always part of practice. However, often athletes are not aware of these processes nor does the coach instruct them. Besides, this would not be practicable in any playing situation in practice or competition. Yet, there are explicit moments during practice that are used for motion-specific and non-motion-specific decision-making learning. Usually the contents of decision-making practice are filed under the tag of tactics or strategies. In the past, the term strategies was used when general precompetitive information and requirements were conveyed (e.g., defensive playing at home or away), whereas the term tactics referred to situation-specific problem solving. Over the years this distinction has been abandoned (see Chandler, 1996; Gréhaigne, Godbout and Bouthier, 1999, for a discussion). Today strategies merely refer to the process of prestructuring option selection and generation in sports games. Tactics, however, refer to individual what- and how-decisions within a particular situation, often simple such as where and how to put my next serve to the opponents' table in table tennis.

Non-motion-specific types of practice

Non-motion-specific types of practice are divided into video-based training, tactics board training and written information on single and group tactical knowledge.

Video-based training

A popular way to prepare oneself for the next opponent or to analyse one's decision-making behaviour is video-based analysis. Coaches or coaching assistants use video clips and sequences of the opposing team or individual players to reveal strengths and weaknesses on single, group and team tactical levels. At this time, there are several simultaneous feedback systems in use that allow for feedback on tactical decision making during practice. The software SIMI VidBack enables a coach to record the whole practice session using a digital video camera and a laptop to replay certain sequences with a time shift of 1 to 30 seconds without stopping the recording at all. This means that, for simple exercises, athletes can observe their own behaviour or motion and can immediately correct it during the practice session. To date these systems have only been employed for technical training and are quite simple – similar to dancing in front of a mirror. As far as we know, no empirical studies on their tactical use have been published. Nevertheless, similar feedback methods are in use for tactical training, for example, in table tennis (see Raab, Masters and Maxwell, 2005).

Tactics board training

Tactics boards are very common in competitive volleyball where coaches use them in time-outs to jot down combinations and moves that the players are expected to execute in the remaining game time. In practice sessions, coaches use tactics boards between the practice sections to present particular team and group formations as well as tactical instructions. According to sport textbooks, it is if–then rules that come into action here. If–then rules contain a situation (if) and an action (then), for example, the following volleyball instruction given to a defender: 'IF the attacking player stretches his arm and just lunges slightly, the ball will be played close to the net. THEN you have to go forward to defend'. There are numerous textbooks devoted exclusively to such if–then rules (see Griffin, Mitchell and Oslin, 1997). The effectiveness of such if–then rules will be covered later in full detail.

Written information

Whereas chess players are known for acquiring most of their knowledge from various chess books and competitions, athletes are supposed to learn primarily by practice. In the wake of rising technological standards, though, parts of the training, such as the preparation phase for a contest, are dedicated to reading written content, resulting in better and faster processing of useful information. One reason is the fact that in Europe nowadays, as in the United States, statistics on nearly any opponent team or player can be gathered daily from the media. In Germany, the Institute for Applied Movement Science (IAT) supports national teams with huge databases and analyses of the worldwide status quo in all sports. Today the problem is often how to decide what and how much information should be given to the athletes. To our knowledge, there has not yet been any systematic research programme investigating the effectiveness of written information in tactical training.

Motion-specific types of practice

Even though non-motion-specific practice types are more important for tactical training than for technical training, the main emphasis within tactical training is on motion-specific practice types (Farrow and Raab, 2008). Motion-specific practice types can be categorized according to the usual taxonomy of teaching models. The dimension incidentally/intentionally distinguishes between self-directed and playful learning (incidental) on one end and coach-specific learning (intentional) that makes the trainee aware of the practice goals and requirements (e.g., if–then rules) on the other. However, comparative studies investigating these teaching models on an internally valid base are the exception rather than the rule. A clear assignment of the various teaching models to either incidental or intentional can only be done near the extremes of the dimension.

Incidental decision-making training

Decision-making training, which is predominantly motion-specific, complies with the underlying simple principle that athletes are expected to gain as much experience in their sport as possible. There are different approaches to such training. Memmert and Roth (2007), for instance, proposed simplifying sports games by easing technical requirements. In this way, players could be exposed to the overall idea of the game very early in learning. In their ball school concept, practice games and competitive games take different forms. Even experts' sayings like 'playing makes perfect' come into play to underline the importance of free play in the development of expertise.

Another approach to improving athletes' decision making is rooted in the research of implicit learning (Masters, 2000). Withholding the original learning objectives and supporting an indirect attention focus on relevant players and game set-ups create implicit learning processes for decision making in sports. Raab (2003) showed that implicit decision-making training in basketball, volleyball and handball produces better decisions in simple decision-making situations than explicit training (see Bertrand and Thullier, 2009; Votsis *et al.*, 2009 for conceptual replications). Participants in this study had to watch video sequences. An implicit group was instructed to take part in a purported memory test that supposedly tested defenders' memory. They had to memorize where a specially tagged player on the video passed the ball. After the presentation of ten video sequences, they had to name either the first five or the last five passes. The presented situations on video have been manipulated in such a way that the attacking team was successful if its players correctly used one of four different if–then rules but failed if they chose an option (if rule) that was not assigned to a corresponding situation by experts. An explicit group was instructed to use four if–then rules, which were presented verbally and visually. All 200 video sequences were identical in the two groups. Groups only differed in the type of instruction. At the end of the acquisition phase, participants were presented another 50 video sequences, stopping right before the tagged player was about to make his or her decision. Participants were then asked to give the best option as quickly as possible.

As mentioned before, results showed that, despite less verbalizable knowledge on correct if–then rules, the implicit group produced better and, in some cases, even faster decisions than the explicit group. In general, there were a significant number of correct decisions in both groups and both groups did better than a control group that received no training at all. The superiority of non-verbalizable rule structures in tactical decision making was confirmed by different studies of the effects of practice in handball, basketball and volleyball. For instance, students were put into different practice groups and received four weeks of practice in tactical decision training either by indirect learning of rules or by practical use of if–then rules (see Raab, 2003). Results indicate that decisions improve in laboratory and field by both incidental and intentional training methods.

Intentional decision-making training

Intentional decision-making training is distinguished by being coach directed. Coaches often prefer this type of training, which can include non-motion-specific instruction and the use of tactics boards. The application of if–then rules taught by visual and verbal demonstration is a central point in this intentional approach (McPherson, 1999). Moreover, the different mechanisms that form a tactical decision together are investigated separately. Griffin, Mitchell and Oslin (1997) suggested separating perception (what information is relevant), option choice (which option is most effective) and motor execution (how the option is executed). Therefore, this approach is quite different from playful teaching methods in incidental decision-making training. Experimental studies in the laboratory (Raab, 2003) and practice studies in the gymnasium (Raab, 2001) indicated that incidental decision-making training is more effective in non-complex situations, whereas intentional decision-making training produces better decisions in complex situations. In these studies complexity varied regarding cognition and perception. On the cognitive level, non-complex situations were defined by four options and four if–then rules and complex situations featured five or more options and twelve to fifteen if–then rules. Consequently, in the latter case participants had to choose the same option in three different situations. Raab (2002) modified the level of complexity by adjusting the number of participating players and their spatial–temporal relation.

So far, we described a number of different models that explain decision-making processes in sports and we presented a number of different decision-making training tools. We now finally give a framework that summarizes and integrates that knowledge.

A framework model for tactical decision-making training

Regarding the 'techniques of tactical training', there have yet to be any systematic listings of recommendations (see Farrow and Raab, 2008, for an overview). These techniques are deduced from empirical models that have been constructed to describe tactical learning and decision-making processes (e.g., SMART: Situation Model of Anticipated Response consequences in Tactical decisions, Raab, 2003; see Raab, 2007 for alternative models).

SMART focuses on implicit or explicit analysis in real situations. Thus, it represents components of perception and verbalizable knowledge during the recognition process within a particular situation. Recognized cues are then extracted from the visual field and used in option generation and choice. Only a few important bits of information are required to generate a few but situation-appropriate options that result in the decision maker choosing the first or at least one of the first options generated. Perceived effects (such as scoring a goal) resulting from a particular decision are used to adapt the subsequent option choice (to a higher degree), option generation (to a lower degree) and situational perception (only in case of continuous failure). Some possible sources of error in common coaching practices, which are not compatible with SMART ideas, will be elucidated in the following.

Sources of error in coaching practices

Source 1: Tactical training is not technical training

The first source of error is a common misperception in sport, namely, that technical and tactical training are two conceptually separate and methodologically independent forms of practice. With its theoretical underpinnings, SMART makes clear that technical training applies to how an action is performed, whereas tactical training addresses what kind of action is most appropriate in a specific situation. This is why SMART argues for practicing technical aspects as a kind of functional contributor to decision making. From a methodological perspective, this could involve isolating complex techniques or their components. However, there is a necessary link between how (technical) and what (tactical) that precludes any isolated form of technical training. Lack of attention to this link can often be seen in very sophisticated technical training settings and preparations that just do not seem to have any effect in real game situations. However, if one considers technical aspects to be a function of the execution of anticipated consequences of actions and tactical aspects to be a situation-appropriate choice from a set of options, then these two aspects should be trained together whenever possible (Raab, Masters and Maxwell, 2005; Vickers, 2007).

Source 2: Tactical training means acquiring tactical knowledge

Too often, one can see coaches giving torrents of tactical speeches, presenting set-ups on tactics boards or positioning players on the field. There are several general and sport-specific approaches to training which explicitly rely on such coaching strategies (see Vickers, 2007). In addition, some coaches still think that only verbalizable knowledge enables athletes on the field to act in a tactically proper way (see McPherson, 1999). Yet, when the role of implicit control mechanisms is understood it becomes clear that athletes are able to solve situations very well because they are good at minimizing the discrepancy between actual and anticipated consequences. The coach's verbal instructions may not necessarily add much. Incidental practice forms, as described earlier, support implicit learning processes (Masters, 2008).

Source 3: Tactical training is subject to the primacy of one method

To put it simply, many coaches believe that if you want to learn technique, then practice; if you want to learn the game, then play. There is even a kind of teaching competition on which method is best to teach which component. However, this way of thinking does not help the training of situation-specific decision making (what and how), because the complexity of a task remains untouched. This is why SMART supports a situation-specific approach that offers multiple methods. Given that the pre-assumptions are accepted, there will be corresponding techniques for the tactical training and tactics for the technical training. First, techniques refer to the different functions of the tactical training, which are represented by the use of implicit and explicit processes. Second, they refer to the coach's possibilities to intervene by changing situations or giving instructions. In the following, the focus is put on five techniques for implementing the search for possibilities, requirements and rules for tactical training, and to separate them by descriptions of the situation and specific instructions:

Technique 1: Search = Practice implicit processes!

Technique 2: Possibilities = Practice explicit processes!

Technique 3: Requirements = Practice explicit in complex situations!

Technique 4: Rules = Practice incidentally first and then intentionally!

Technique 5: Tactical training = Practice divergent and convergent solutions!

Technique 1: Search = Practice implicit processes!

According to the idea of Technique 1, training situations are expected to give athletes the necessary experience to separate relevant from irrelevant situational cues. In sports games, for example, a defender depends on realizing relevant characteristics of attacking moves to anticipate the direction of attack. Situations that make, for instance, a handball goalkeeper distinguish very early between a direct throw and a lob produce indirect attention direction, which the athlete needs to meet situational requirements (Raab, 2002). Researchers in handball (Memmert and Roth, 2007) as well as in volleyball (Raab, 2003) have suggested that such situations do not necessarily have to be practiced independently of the athlete's individual actions. In particular, perception-specific situations, featuring primarily indirect attention direction, are widespread in training concepts among modern sports games, such as streetball, beach football or beach volleyball. Play-oriented methodological approaches with holistic perspective or game simulations offer a perfect learning environment for practicing implicit processes.

Instructions are only expected to contain viewing direction and strategies, because these information sources are sufficient for the athlete to solve a specific problem. In volleyball, for example, it is not movement instruction (if 'stretched arm' then 'lob'; if 'deep lunge' then 'strike') but situational information (if 'attacker hits the ball' look to 'the side of the striking arm') that is appropriate to anticipate the attacker's different actions (lob or strike). To sum up, the focus on play-oriented methodical approaches and situation-specific instructions distinguishes Technique 1 from any other classical form of perception training.

Technique 2: Possibilities = Practice explicit processes!

Training situations should be created according to the number of options, their emphasis, their probability of occurrence and other relevant attributes. In basketball, only the winger's options 'shoot' and 'pass to the point guard' can be linked to the greater importance of scoring. Furthermore, the wing player only has to consider the distance to his defender. Further variations in time pressure, influence of prior experience and scoring requirements will also increase the consideration of additional possible decision-making parameters. Definitions should not be exclusively limited to probabilities and action alternatives though. At the same time, the choice between incidental and intentional teaching concepts depends on other factors, as does complexity (see Technique 3) and teaching order (see Technique 4) such as expertise of the athletes, content and goal of the training.

Due to different training situations the probability of success and valence of a trained decision can be directly linked to its consequences. There is no need for long speeches or statistical tables of success and valence. Although the coach does need this information, it should not be passed on to the athletes in this form. Instead, instructions should refer to solutions of specific situations taking the probability of success into account. Technique 2 adds time pressure and instructions for situation solutions to the 'classical training of goal formation'.

Technique 3: Requirements = Practice in a complexity-specific way!

Efficient employment of incidental and intentional teaching models depends on the complexity of the specific situation. Incidental teaching models are preferably used for simple situational settings characterized by minimal explicit processes (such as fewer options, fewer attributes and less weighing) and structured implicit processes (such as extremely divergent environmental conditions). On the other hand, particular requirements in complex situations should trigger intentional teaching units. Following training schedules lasting several weeks, situations should be gradually increased in complexity depending on the skill level of the training group. Consequently, emphasis on incidental and intentional methods has to be shifted accordingly (see Technique 4). For this reason it is helpful to classify the different teaching models according to the incidental–intentional dimension (see Raab, 2007).

With incidental teaching models, instructions should be directed towards the possible number of options. With intentional models, however, possible gaze strategies and action alternatives have to be limited by providing directions towards information sources (implicit, see Technique 1) and possible options (explicit, see Technique 2). Whereas Techniques 1 and 2 only differ in the accentuation of the underlying conceptual methods, Technique 3 demands an explicit change of tactical training.

Technique 4: Rules = Practice incidentally first and then intentionally!

To achieve effective implicit and explicit rule formation, teaching models are not only expected to be complexity-specific but also set up in well-structured combinations. Only after having acquired incidental experience should athletes be exposed to intentional training methods that help structure situations. This is why we discourage doing it the other way around by starting out with verbal or visual explicit rule formation.

Instructions should be built on the connection between initially learned incidental experiences and subsequently acquired explicit experiences. The more complex a specific situation is, the more important is the emphasis of that connection between previous experience and the selection between a huge array of provided options (see Technique 3). Therefore, the explicit processes should outweigh implicit processes because pure implicit processes do not allow solving the complex choice (see Technique 1). Technique 4 dictates the order of teaching methods: first implicit then explicit. Instructions for rule formation should also consider implicit experience.

Technique 5: Tactical training = Practice divergent and convergent solutions!

A major function of tactical training is to teach the athlete how to generate a pool of possible action alternatives (divergent options) and to choose the most effective one for a specific situation out of this pool of options (convergent options). Divergent tasks are used to improve the athlete's creative choice and the number of options to consider, which are best performed by incidental teaching models. Enhancing the athlete's creative tactical behaviour is not simply 'playing'. The coach's job is to create situations that force the athlete to generate, choose and use required action alternatives (Johnson and Raab, 2003). Additionally, external motivational incentives such as a 'creativity bonus' or similar incentives are also useful. Choosing the most effective action alternative is best taught by intentional teaching methods, if Techniques 3 and 4 do not clash with it.

Instructions with divergent tasks have to connect to the generating criteria. That is, the coach has to simulate useful action alternatives which are possible within any offence setting (handball, basketball), rotation (volleyball) or set piece (football). Regarding convergent tasks, the athletes should always evaluate all possible options afterwards. In contrast to a 'classical' decision-making training, Technique 5 emphasizes if–then rules in formats such as if–if–if . . . if–then or if–then–then–then . . . then.

Summarizing SMART, the main suggestion is to practice situation solutions by analysing perceived information and choosing an adequate action that corresponds to it. There is nothing new to this approach, since perception and cognition have had to be practiced ever since the development of competitions in sport. The five techniques of tactical training, however, focus on when and how incidental and intentional learning environments have to be effectively combined when considering task complexity. Note that this will not automatically lead to complete success in competition. Experience tells us that any ever-so-perfectly trained tactical solution first and foremost has to be put into action on the field.

SUMMARY

For short-term decisions we considered the following aspects.

1 *Perception and memory*. How early information is perceived as well as system limitations influence decision making. Thus, exposure through practice to system-specific limitation and performance within

realistic situations is preferred to exclusive visual and perceptual training. Experts' and novices' memory performances in sports only differ in sport-specific and action-specific situations. This is why even in the early years of an athlete's career recognition and reproduction skills have to be practiced sport- and situation-specifically.

2 *Attention and concentration.* Divided as well as focused attention are both variably employed on a situation- and personality-specific level. Selection of task-specific information works better in experts than in novices because expertise directs early attention to important information and corresponding actions correlate directly with the perceived information.

3 *Decision-making processes.* Decision-making processes relate to option generation (Which options do I have?) and option choice (Which option will I take?). Option choice distinguishes between 'what' decisions and 'how' decisions. Experts produce fewer and better options than novices.

4 *Coping strategies.* Coping strategies are an important component of setting the stage for decision-making processes. Problem-oriented and emotion-oriented strategies can be separated and personal as well as situational variables influence the specific coping strategies and their positive influence on the decision-making process.

For the long-term decisions and the development of decision making we considered (i) doping and career decisions, (ii) expertise – the amount of free play and deliberate play should gradually decrease in the course of learning, whereas the proportion of structured and deliberate practice should increase. Research on specific and general training content is still needed, (iii) decision-making training – there are motion-specific and non-motion-specific practice methods. The various training models differ regarding their amount of verbalizable knowledge and the effectiveness, which depend primarily on situational factors, (iv) SMART – SMART incorporates the aspects and information of all the areas mentioned above. SMART serves as a means to test and teach decision making in theory and practice.

Managers and Coaches

6

Managers and Coaches

JDM AS A LEADERSHIP TASK

Managers and coaches are usually considered as (two kinds of) leaders, as reflected by the existing literature on leadership in sport (see, for review, Chelladurai, 2007). Since the early days of research on behaviour in organizations (e.g., Barnard, 1938), it is evident that in order to excel as a leader, a person should enhance his or her JDM skills. Successful leadership – including effective JDM processes – is therefore considered a key determinant of any organizational success (Wood *et al.*, 2004), with sport organizations being no exception (Scott, 1999; Smart and Wolfe, 2003). Accordingly, leadership has been one of the most widely studied concepts in the scientific study of organizational behaviour (André, 2008), including the group dynamics research in both sport management (Chelladurai, 2006) and sport psychology (Carron, Hausenblas and Eys, 2005).

Many definitions of leadership have been suggested, with emphasis placed on important elements such as the ability to guide a group toward the achievement of goals (Riggio, 2003), which is in fact the process whereby an individual influences other group members towards the attainment of group and/or organizational goals (Greenberg and Baron, 2007). Thus, as already proposed towards the end of the 1980s, in both organizational (Kotter, 1990) and sport (Martens, 1987) psychology,

Judgement, Decision Making and Success in Sport, First Edition.
M. Bar-Eli, H. Plessner and M. Raab.
© 2011 John Wiley & Sons, Ltd. Published 2011 by John Wiley & Sons, Ltd.

the primary function of a leader is to provide and establish the fundamental organizational mission (i.e., a vision that helps to determine the direction that the organization or team pursues) and to formulate the strategy for its implementation (i.e., for attaining the goals and objectives derived from that mission).

Managers are sometimes contrasted to leaders as being primarily responsible for implementing the organizational mission and strategy through others (i.e., through increasing employees' commitment and effort, as well as through practicing various organizational functions such as planning, scheduling, budgeting, staffing and recruiting). But the terms 'leader' and 'manager' are quite frequently used interchangeably, among others, because there are several overlapping functions that make the distinction between leaders and managers non-obvious and blurred in actual practice, as noted by Bar-Eli and Schack (2005).

In the sport-leadership literature (see, for review, Chelladurai, 2007), managers and coaches are discussed within the contexts of sport management (Slack and Parent, 2006) and sport psychology (Horn, 2002), respectively. In order to be effective leaders, both should be 'tuned in' to the needs of the organization and/or group members and provide the right balance between task- and relationship-oriented styles in order to strive for excellence through facilitating the performance of their organizations/groups to the maximum required in a given situation (Bar-Eli and Schack, 2005). Thus, the pursuit of excellence, which can be defined – in line with Keating (1964) and Sternberg (1993) – as 'performance at the highest levels within each comparative group of participants ... established through victories in organized competitions' (Chelladurai, 2007, p. 125), is essential to achieve success in sport and requires both managers and coaches to maximize their leadership performances, for example, through optimizing their JDM processes (Bar-Eli, Lowengart et al., 2006). As mentioned above, JDM is considered to be one of the major tasks in which managers and coaches are involved, with some people even arguing that JDM is 'the single most important process in an organization' (Slack and Parent, 2006, p. 258). Effective JDM seems to be essential to the excellence evident in highly successful sport organizations (Bar-Eli, Galily and Israeli, 2008).

In this chapter, we will first overview some classical approaches to JDM, which were initially suggested in reference to (sport) managers. Later on, coaches' JDM will be presented.

MANAGERIAL JDM

Decision types and environments

The process of decision making – considered to be a key element in the life of any organization since the very beginning of management theory (e.g., Barnard, 1938) – occurs as a reaction to a problem (Sanders, 1999). According to Nobel Prize winner Herbert A. Simon (Simon, 1960), managers' decisions can be categorized into programmed and non-programmed types (see also Soelberg, 1966). Programmed decisions are made in response to relatively simple repetitive problems that arise routinely and that can be addressed through standard, clearly defined procedures and policies. Programmed decisions implement routine solutions guided by past experience as appropriate for problems at hand, which are relatively well structured, present clear alternatives whose viability is not too difficult to assess and who have adequate information available.

In contrast, non-programmed decisions are made about non-routine, relatively complex and novel problems, for which there are no pre-established courses of action. Such unique and new problems call for decisions that are created and tailored to deal with specific situations at hand. In this case, decisions are made where there are no established procedures and/or guidelines that may direct the way this type of problem should be handled. There are no clear alternatives from which to select, for example, because the organization has never in the past faced the necessity of handling such problems – a situation which requires making unique and new (i.e., non-programmed) decisions.

It is frequently assumed (see, for example, André, 2008), that programmed decisions – because they are well structured and should follow explicit often written rules – will generally be made by the organization's lower-level managers and operators. In contrast, non-programmable decisions – because of their novel characteristics which lack identifiable rules for developing solutions and, therefore, require the use of (creative) judgement – will more likely be made by upper level, senior managers or highly trained professional staff (see also Nutt, 1993, 2002). It is also assumed (see, for example, Wedley and Field, 1984) that managers attempt to programme the decision making whenever possible, because these choices can be handled by less-qualified, cheaper staff.

As noted by March and his associates (e.g., Cohen, March and Olsen, 1972; March and Simon, 1958), problem-solving decisions in organizations are typically made under three different conditions: certainty, risk and uncertainty. Certain environments provide the decision maker with exact and full information regarding the expected results for the different alternatives at hand, that is, when the manager understands completely the available alternatives and the outcome (costs and benefits) of each. Then the information is sufficient to predict the expected results of each alternative in advance of implementation and the decision environment is considered certain. Certainty is of course an ideal condition for managerial problem solving and decision making, because in this case, the challenge simply is to locate the alternative offering of the best of ideal solutions. Certainty is the exception instead of the rule among decision environments though.

Risk environments – far more common in organizational settings – exist when decision makers lack complete certainty regarding the outcome of various alternative courses of action, but they are aware of the probabilities associated with their occurrence. Probabilities regarding expected results for decision-making alternatives can be assigned through objective statistical procedures or through personal intuition. In other words, the decision maker under risk conditions has in fact a basic understanding of the available alternatives, but is uncertain about the potential costs and benefits associated with each. In such a case, he or she must assign probabilities to the outcome in order to work out the best decision – a process which can be done objectively (i.e., based on available data), but is often done subjectively (i.e., based on one's own past experiences).

Uncertain environments exist when the decision alternatives and their potential outcome are both relatively unknown, for example, due to the lack of either historical data and/or past experiences on which a decision can be made. Here, then, managers have so little information on hand that they cannot even assign probabilities to various alternatives and their possible outcomes. This is the most difficult of the three decision environments, because uncertainty forces decision makers to rely heavily on individual and/or group creativity, among others, to succeed in problem solving. Uncertainty often requires unique, novel and innovative alternatives to existing patterns of behaviour, with the decision maker being heavily influenced by intuition, educated guesses and hunches. In some cases, an uncertain decision environment may also be characterized as an 'organized anarchy'. This can be characterized as a rapidly changing organizational setting in terms of external conditions, the information technology requirements called for to analyse and to make decisions and the personnel influencing problem and choice definitions.

Decision-making models

From an historical perspective, the field of organizational behaviour traditionally emphasized two basic alternative models of individual decision making, namely the classical-rational and the administrative-behavioural (Simon, 1945). The classical-rational model of decision making assumes that the manager faces a clearly defined problem, that he knows all possible action alternatives and their consequences, and then chooses the alternative that offers the best or 'optimum' solution to the problem. However, this optimizing style is an ideal – rather than real – way to make decisions, because it actually views the manager as acting in a world of complete certainty. In fact, it is normative and prescriptive, being based on postulates that enable one's optimal maximization of gain and minimization of loss (for reviews, see Baron, 2004, 2008); as such, it is more a model for how decisions should be (rather than how they really are) made (cf. Chapter 3, Subjective expected utility theory).

In sport management, Slack and Parent (2006) depicted such a model as a series of steps in the decision-making process, which are based on the premise that sport managers act analytically in an economically rational way. In line with several other authors (e.g., Archer, 1980), they suggested the following steps: monitor the decision environment, define the problem about which a decision has to be made, diagnose the problem, identify decision alternatives, analyse alternatives, select the best alternative, implement the chosen alternative and evaluate the decision made (see also Nutt, 1993, 2002; Wedley and Field, 1984). From a more general perspective, prescriptive-analytical models of managerial decision making (see, for review, Huczynski and Buchanan, 2007), which recommend how individuals should behave in order to achieve a desired outcome, are usually based on scientific principles, empiricism and positivism as well as on the use of decision criteria of evidence, logical argument and reasoning (Langley, 1989).

Despite the inherent logic of the systematic approach outlined in the classical-rational model, managers are rarely this thorough or precise in their real, everyday decision behaviour. The limitations of the classical-rational model were first identified by Simon (1945, 1955), who drew a distinction between the major principles of economics and what happens in everyday life. He suggested that organizational decision making was bounded by the limited cognitive ability to process information of the managers involved by their emotions and by factors such as imperfect information and time constraints. Hence, managers – rather than being completely rational in the classical sense – operate in reality with what Simon (1955, 1956) referred to as bounded rationality. In any decision situation a manager has a limited perception; he or she cannot really understand all the available alternatives and even if he/she does, the limits of the human mind would not allow all that information to be processed. In addition, human rationality is constrained by the manager's subjective experience and emotions.

It is usually assumed that classical-rational decision theory does not appear to fit the current somewhat chaotic world of globalizing high-tech organizations. However, as noted, for example, by Schermerhorn, Hunt and Osborn (2003), it would be a mistake to dismiss it completely, including the types of progress that can be made with classical-rational models. Such models, for example, can be used towards the bottom of many organizations; for instance, even the most advanced high-tech firm faces many clearly defined problems with known alternatives where firms have already selected an optimal solution. Furthermore, Bar-Eli, Lowengart et al. (2006) recently suggested not to abandon the old principle of 'maximization through optimization' – a principle that is central among the major aspects of human rationality required in sport for the pursuit of excellence (Bar-Eli, Lurie and Breivik, 1999). Along these lines, several methods have been proposed to aid the optimization of people's thought processes in elite sport, such as the Bayesian approach (see, for a review, Tenenbaum and Bar-Eli, 1993). Risk-taking strategies in sport were analysed within a transactional framework, suggesting ways of improving the decision maker's accuracy (Bar-Eli, 2001, 2002). Studies in management science, particularly in operations research, demonstrated that sport psychology could indeed be provided with rational models that have the potential of being used as effective optimization aids for performance maximization (Mehrez et al., 2006; Sinuany-Stern, Israeli and Bar-Eli, 2006).

Such an approach reflects rationality in its instrumental sense, which has to do with the effectiveness of one's application of means towards the accomplishment of a certain goal (Weber, 1946). Instrumental rationality and/or reasoning are reflected, for example, not only in the current literature on expert sport performance – with special reference to the 'deliberate practice' paradigm (see, for review, Ericsson, 1996b, 2003) – and in the professionalization processes of organized elite sport (Coakley, 2006), but also in the systematic reproductions approach to creativity – labelled by Bar-Eli, Lowengart et al. (2006), as 'optimized creativity' – which attempts to identify an optimal course of action which will most probably bring about the best solution to a given problem, thereby actually applying the 'maximization through optimization' principle for producing creative processes.

At any rate, the area of managerial JDM has been heavily 'psychologized' since the introduction of the bounded rationality concept by Simon (1955, 1956), turning its major focus to the administrative-behavioural model of decision making, which resulted in a systematic, descriptive characterization of how real people actually behave. Over the years, the concept of bounded rationality became quite synonymous with the study of heuristics and biases, thus underpinning classical rationality as a normative standard (for a critical review, see Lopes, 1991, 1992). Consequently, the JDM psychology has focused on the gaps between the ideal (i.e., normative) and real (i.e., descriptive) facets of JDM, in an attempt to understand their causes; such comparisons between normative and descriptive aspects of JDM have also been conducted in sports contexts, although not that frequently (see, for example, Gröschner and Raab, 2006). Currently, JDM is conceived to a large degree in terms of human information processing and is mostly regarded as part of cognitive and social psychology – as is evident from the different approaches to JDM included in Koehler and Harvey (2004).

The major perspective evident within the current research on human JDM heuristics is the 'judgement under uncertainty' programme of Kahneman, Tversky and others (see, for review, Gilovich, Griffin and Kahneman, 2002). This stimulating research programme emerged from the earlier research on human information processing conducted by Edwards and his co-workers (e.g., Edwards, 1962, 1968; Edwards, Lindman and Savage, 1963), who proposed Bayesian statistics for scientific hypothesis evaluation and considered the human mind as a reasonably good, albeit conservative, Bayesian statistician. In fact, Edwards made a key methodological contribution by introducing Bayesian analyses to psychology, thus providing a normative standard with which everyday judgements could be compared. From Edwards's own research and others' research (especially Simon's abovementioned work), it became clear that intuitive judgements of likelihood did not exactly correspond with this 'ideal' normative standard. This led, in turn, to an interest in the causes of suboptimal performance and strategies for improvement, with the 'judgement under uncertainty' programme investigating reasoning as intuitive statistics, focusing mainly on errors in probabilistic reasoning.

The central idea of the 'heuristics and biases' programme, namely, that judgement under uncertainty often rests on a limited number of simplifying heuristics rather than on extensive algorithmic processing, revolutionized academic research on human JDM. It soon spread – following a series of papers published by Tversky and Kahneman mainly in the late 1960s and early 1970s (see, for review, Kahneman, Slovic and Tversky, 1982) – across a range of disciplines including not only psychology, but also many more, such as management, economics, law, medicine and political science. Despite some apparent critics and oppositions, for example, by the so-called 'ecological rationality movement', evident mainly by Gigerenzer's (2000, 2004) 'fast-and-frugal-heuristics' approach which was recently applied also in sport (see Bennis and Pachur, 2006), the 'heuristics and biases' perspective reached its peak with the Nobel Prize awarded in 2002 to Daniel Kahneman for his work conducted jointly with the late Amos Tversky.

As a result of these developments, the organizational behaviour literature increasingly recognized the central role of intuition as a key element in making non-programmed decisions under risk and uncertainty (e.g., Agor, 1989; Andersen, 2000; Khatri and Ng, 2000; Myers, 2002; Plessner, Betsch and Betsch, 2008). Recent organizational behaviour textbooks (e.g., André, 2008; Huczynski and Buchanan, 2007; Schermerhorn, Hunt and Osborn, 2003; Wood *et al.*, 2004) usually discuss judgemental heuristics and creativity factors as two major components of human intuition, but almost none of this has been reflected in the sport management or sport psychology literature (as noted by Bar-Eli and Raab, 2006a). This state of affairs is quite surprising because in 1985, for example, one of the most provocative studies in the history of JDM was published, namely Gilovich, Vallone and Tversky's (1985) investigation of the misperception of the 'hot hand' in basketball, which was a part of the stimulating research programme on heuristics and biases. Gilovich, Vallone and Tversky (1985) were interested in studying deeply rooted misconceptions – that is, beliefs that are neither compatible with normative considerations based on paradigmatic reasoning models, nor with the real physical world – which may dominate human JDM behaviour. For that purpose, they demonstrated how the use of the representativeness heuristic (Tversky and Kahneman, 1982) might lead to deficient perceptions of random events during top-level athletic events, such as NBA basketball games. For instance, in the Gilovich, Vallone and Tversky (1985) 'Study 1' they asked fans in basketball to estimate the probability of the next shoot of an average player with a shooting percentage of 50% for field goals (or 70% for free throws) if this player just missed (cold hand) or scored (hot hand) two or three balls. Figure 6.1 shows that fans believe in a positive dependence between successive shots even if a number of studies cannot support such a dependency (but see Burns, 2004). Despite the great theoretical and practical potential for sport management and sport psychology, these findings were to a large degree disregarded in the relevant literature, although recently, sport psychologists have become increasingly interested in these phenomena (see, for a review, Bar-Eli, Avugos and Raab, 2006).

A similar state of affairs can be observed for creativity. In sport, creativity is considered a prerequisite for enhanced performance (Bar-Eli, 1991; Bar-Eli, Lurie and Breivik, 1999; Morris, 2000). However, research in the area of sport management has been primarily descriptive, without being closely linked theoretically and/or empirically to the

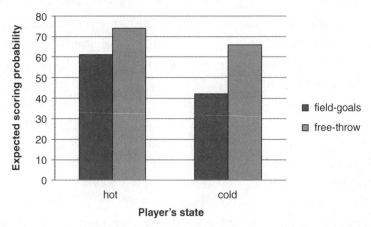

Figure 6.1 Fans' average estimate of a player's goal percentage 'after having just made a shot' (hot) and 'after having just missed a shot' (cold) in basketball (Gilovich *et al.*, 1985).

large body of the general and/or sport-specific literature. For example, whereas early researchers (e.g., Loy, 1981) investigated the personality characteristics of sport innovators, others have proposed various techniques for enhancing athletes' creativity (e.g., Mirvis, 1998; Piirto, 1998; Ringrose, 1993) or have examined the effects of such techniques on athletes' performance (e.g., Everhart *et al.*, 1999; Hanin *et al.*, 2002). It was suggested that sports practitioners use creative, psychological interventions in order to cope with these problems; more specifically, it was recommended that in sports organizations, creativity-enhancement methods (see Bar-Eli, 1991; Schmole, 2000) should be integrated into practitioners' mental (e.g., judgement and decision) models to increase their effectiveness by promoting the creation of knowledge through second-order change processes (Stacey, 2007). Although contemporary sport management educators believe that future sport managers will (increasingly) need exceptional skills of critical thinking (Edwards, 1999; Keeley and Parks, 2003), such issues are quite rare in the current sport management literature (or, at the most, marginally discussed – if at all – within the framework of organizational change; see, for example, Slack and Parent, 2006).

To rectify this situation, Bar-Eli and his associates initiated a series of studies on heuristics and biases (Azar and Bar-Eli, 2008; Bar-Eli, Avugos and Raab, 2006; Bar-Eli and Azar, 2009; Bar-Eli *et al.*, 2007) and creativity (Bar-Eli, Lowengart *et al.*, 2006; Bar-Eli, Lowengart *et al.*, 2008; Goldenberg *et al.*, 2004; Goldenberg *et al.*, 2010) in sport. Although they are also relevant for sport-managerial JDM, we will present these studies later in this chapter, when discussing coaches' JDM processes.

Group and organizational decisions

To understand behaviour in sport organizations fully, we must consider processes occurring within individuals, groups and organization systems. These are often referred to as the three 'levels' or 'units' of analysis (e.g., Greenberg and Baron, 2007; Robbins, 2005) used in organizational behaviour. Thus far, managerial JDM was discussed here mainly on the individual level; in what follows, group and organizational decision processes will be briefly reviewed.

Outside the realm of sport, scientific research on groups has traditionally focused on topics such as group cohesion, conformity, composition, decision making, development, formation, leadership, motivation, size, structure, and tasks as well as intergroup relations (Parks and Sanna, 1999; Stewart, Manz and Sims, 1998). In sport and exercise settings, some of these topics have been investigated more extensively, such as cohesion, leadership, size and composition (see, for review, Bar-Eli and Schack, 2005), but not (J)DM (Raab and Reimer, 2007). Group decisions are very common and well established in modern organizational life (Davis, 1992). Therefore, one major question would be, under what conditions groups or individuals might be expected to make superior decisions.

Research conducted already in the 1980s and 1990s (e.g., Gigone and Hastie, 1997; Hill, 1982; Wanous and Youtz, 1986; Yetton and Bottger, 1983) indicated that, when performing complex problems, groups were superior to individuals if certain conditions prevailed, for example when members had heterogeneous and complementary skills, when they could freely share ideas and when their (good) ideas were accepted by others. However, when performing simple problems, groups performed only as well as the best individual group member – and then only, if that person had the correct answer and if that answer was accepted by others in the group. It was also found that groups performed worse than individuals when working on poorly structured, creative tasks. A great part of the problem seemed to be that some individuals felt inhibited by the presence of others, even though one rule of brainstorming (which is a technique designed to foster group productivity by encouraging interacting group members to express their ideas in a non-critical fashion; see Bouchard, Barsaloux and Drauden, 1974), for example, is that even far-out ideas may be shared. Their creativity may be inhibited when in groups to the extent that people wish to avoid feeling foolish as a result of 'saying silly things'. Similarly, groups may inhibit creativity by slowing down the process of bringing ideas to fruition.

It can be surmised that on the one hand, groups are a source of both breadth and depth of input for information gathering. If the group is composed of persons with diverse backgrounds, the alternatives generated should be more extensive and the analysis more critical. Reimer, Park and Hinsz (2006) maintained that shared cognition is crucial to the understanding of team performance. According to these authors, the degree to which cognitions are shared and coordinated among team members substantially affects the extent to which individual actions are effectively coordinated. Moreover, when a final solution is agreed upon, there are more people in a group decision to support and actively implement it.

In contrast to that, these advantages can be offset by the time group decisions consume, by the internal conflicts they create, and by the pressures they generate towards conformity. Two notable examples of such drawbacks are the well-known phenomena of groupshift (i.e., a change in decision risk between the group's and the individual's decision that members within the group would make, which can be either towards conservatism or greater risk; see, for example, Isenberg, 1986; Paese, Bieser and Tubbs, 1993), and groupthink (i.e., when the norm for consensus overrides the realistic appraisal of alternative courses of action; see, for example, Choi and Kim, 1999; Janis, 1982; Park, 1990). Such phenomena – and group (J)DM in general – should be further investigated in the realm of sport management to promote our understanding of organizational behaviour in this setting.

On the organization systems level, studies of managerial decision making have identified five major approaches: management science, the Carnegie model, the structuring of 'unstructured' processes, the garbage can model and Bradford studies. Despite the fact that relatively little or no work has made use of most of these approaches in the sport management literature, Slack and Parent (2006), for example, do believe in the necessity of understanding organizational decision processes and the factors influencing them through implementing these approaches in sport management. For this reason, we will briefly review each of these approaches here.

The management science approach was developed during the Second World War. It involved the use of mathematics and statistics to model and solve complex military problems (Leavitt, Dill and Eyring, 1973; Markland, 1989). According to Ladany (2006), the first studies of management science in sport were purely descriptive and they were on cricket. The first optimization studies were performed in the late 1950s and early 1960s. Many of these were applied to baseball, but also to other sports, such as light athletics (track and field), basketball, hockey, golf, weightlifting, rowing, swimming and tennis, in an attempt to improve performances and/or to maximize the probabilities of success. Concurrently, league scheduling problems and ranking issues of teams and individuals were investigated and improved. The publication of articles dealing with quantitative approaches to analyse and improve sports' activities reached its maturity in the middle of the 1970s (e.g., Ladany and Machol, 1977; Machol, Ladany and Morrison, 1976), and it has continued until the present (see, for review, Ladany, 2006). Despite these efforts, decisions in sport organizations can further profit from management science (Slack and Parent, 2006).

The Carnegie Model (introduced first by Cyert and March, 1963) conceived organizational decision making as a political process and extended Simon's (1955, 1956, 1960) concept of bounded rationality by challenging the idea that an organization makes rational decisions as a single entity. These authors argued that organizations are actually made up of subunits with diverse interests – a state of affairs that results in organization-level decisions based on coalitions between managers. Since these managers have a bounded rationality, that is, they do not always have the cognitive ability or time to deal with all aspects of every problem, decisions are frequently split into subproblems – a process which often leads to coalition building. As a consequence, there is a continuous bargaining process among the various groups and/or sub-units in the organization, with managers often spending more time on managing coalitions and resolving internal conflicts than on managing the actual problems to be solved. On the individual level, managers' bounded rationality leads them to a quick search of satisficing solutions, which often reflect the short-term interests of their respective subunits rather than a long-term strategy, which is best for the entire organization.

In their 'structuring the "unstructured"' approach, Mintzberg, Raisinghani and Théorêt (1976) focused on decisions made at the senior organizational levels in an attempt to identify the structure of the supposedly 'unstructured' process of strategic decision making. These authors suggested that major decisions in an organization are in fact broken down into smaller decisions which collectively contribute to the major decision. They proposed to divide the decision process into three major phases (identification, development and selection), with each phase containing different routines (seven in total). According to Mintzberg, Raisinghani and Théorêt (1976), the decision process is also characterized by interruptions, which are events that result in a change in the direction or pace of the decision process. Interruptions cause delays because they force an organization to go back and modify its solution, find another one or engage in political activity to remove an obstacle. Each of these three phases, the routines they contain and the respective interruptions are required to structure major decisions made in organizations, and the model as a whole has considerable potential for being applied in sport management (Slack and Parent, 2006).

The garbage can model (Cohen, March and Olsen, 1972) suggested that contrary to the assumption that some logical sequence can usually be observed in DM processes, the reality is much more complex and confusing – a situation referred to as 'organized anarchy'. According to this view, decision making in organizations operating in rapidly changing environments would be an outcome of four independent streams of events (i.e., problems, choice opportunities, participants and solutions), which actually means that the process of decision making would be somewhat random. The organization is described here as a 'garbage can' into which problems, choices, participants and solutions are all placed, with managers having to act, facing a high amount of disorder, making decisions that are rarely systematic and logical and choices that are made, when problems come together with participants and solutions. As a consequence, some problems are never really solved, solutions are put forward even when a problem has yet to be identified and choices are made before problems are understood. In short, this model draws attention to the role of chance and timing in the decision-making process. In addition – unlike other approaches, which tend to focus on single decisions – it is concerned primarily with multiple decisions.

The Bradford studies – so named because they were conducted at the University of Bradford in the UK by Hickson and his research team (e.g., Cray *et al.*, 1988, 1991; Hickson *et al.*, 1985, 1986) – focused on the decision-making process (as opposed to the outcome and implementation of the decisions made) and identified five dimensions of process (which encompass 12 variables): scrutiny, interaction, flow, duration and authority. In reference to these dimensions and variables, they identified three distinct ways of making decisions, which were labelled 'sporadic', 'fluid' and 'constricted' processes. According to Slack and Parent (2006), the dimensions, variables and processes proposed by the Bradford approach enjoy considerable acceptance in the general field of management and should therefore be replicated and extended in the realm of sport to understand organizational decision making better in this setting.

It can be concluded that almost no work in the sport management literature has made use of these five major approaches to organizational decision making (probably, with the exception of management science, as was demonstrated above). Thus, investigating these approaches in sport organizations can enhance the understanding of decision processes in such organizations, extend existing theory on this topic and contribute to management research in general.

COACHES' JDM

Decision styles

Coaches' behaviour has been investigated mainly within two major thrusts of leadership studies: Smoll and Smith's (1989) mediational model and Chelladurai's (1990, 1993) multidimensional model.

The mediational model focused on studying the effects of coaching behaviour on young athletes and specified the linkages among coaching behaviours, athletes' perceptions of those behaviours and athletes' evaluative reactions to the experienced coaching behaviours. The model identified situational and individual differences in coaches and athletes, which affected their behaviours, perceptions and evaluative reactions, as well as the linkages among them (Smoll and Smith, 1989). The model also guided some methods for measuring variables considered important in studying coaches' behaviour in youth sport, such as Smith, Smoll and Hunt's (1977) behavioural assessment instrument known as CBAS (Coaching Behaviour Assessment System), and/or Smith, Smoll and Curtis's (1978) self-report instruments developed to measure athletes' perceptions of coaching behaviours and their evaluative reactions to the coach, the sport experience and themselves. Much research has been conducted in accordance with the model (R. E. Smith, 1999), but no explicit reference to coaches' JDM behaviour was made within this approach.

Coaches' decision styles were investigated mainly within the broad conceptual framework of the multidimensional model of leadership, which had its origins in sport psychology (Chelladurai, 1990, 1993) and sport management (Chelladurai, 1999). According to this model, leader-, group member- and situational characteristics may produce three states of leader behaviour – actual, preferred and required. The individual differences among the group members and the leader significantly affect the leadership process and its effectiveness, as do the characteristics of the situation. Actual leader behaviour reflects not only the adaptation of the leader to the demands and constraints placed by the situation, but is also a function of his or her responses to group members' preferences. In fact, this model proposed that the degree of congruence among the three states of leader behaviour determines the extent to which group members are not only satisfied, but also successfully perform as individuals and as a group.

Chelladurai (1990, 1993, 1999) incorporated previous theories and research findings from social and organizational psychology into his model of leadership effectiveness. In particular, the multidimensional model of leadership synthesized central concepts such as Fiedler's (1967) contingency model and House's (1971) path–goal theory, both of which emphasize the contingency between the leader and the situation in which he or she operates. More recently, perceived trans-formational leadership was investigated within the extended context of this approach (Kent and Chelladurai, 2001).

To measure the broad, general spectrum of leadership behaviours (e.g., style) in sport, Chelladurai and his associates developed the leadership scale for sports (LSS) towards the end of the 1970s (e.g., Chelladurai and Saleh, 1978, 1980); over the years, LSS has become the most often used instruments to measure coaches' leadership style (Horn, 2002). The LSS includes five subscales: two that measure the coach's decision-making style (democratic and autocratic), two that measure his or her motivational tendencies (social support and positive feedback) and one that measures the coach's instructional behaviour (training and instruction). Items on the two decision-making style factors describe a coach, who allows athletes to participate in decisions about group goals, practice methods and game strategies and tactics (democratic style), and one who is aloof from his or her players and who stresses his or her authority in dealing with them (autocratic style). However, if a measurement is required of the more specific aspect of leadership behaviour, namely, that of decision style, then the decision-style questionnaire developed by Chelladurai and his associates in the mid to late 1980s may be preferable (see, for reviews, Chelladurai, 1993; Chelladurai and Riemer, 1998).

The decision-style questionnaire provides a measure of the coach's decision-making style and is based primarily on a model for decision making in the athletic domain, which was developed by Chelladurai and Haggerty (1978). This model, known as the normative model of decision styles in coaching, was substantially affected by Vroom and Yelton's (1973) comprehensive work on leadership and decision making. In line with Vroom and Yelton, Chelladurai and Haggerty suggested that the particular decision-making style used by a coach in any situation can vary on a continuum which is defined in terms of the amount of participation that group members (i.e., athletes) are allowed to have in the decision process. This continuum can range from an autocratic decision-making style (i.e., the coach alone makes decisions), to a delegative one (i.e., the coach delegates the decisions to be made). Additional points between the two ends represent a consultative decision-making style (i.e., the coach first consults with one or more team members and only then makes decisions) and a participative one (i.e., the coach and one or more team members jointly make decisions).

Chelladurai and Haggerty (1978) proposed that the effectiveness of the various decision-making styles can be predicted by assessing some situational variables, namely, (i) the degree to which the decision is crucial, (ii) the amount of relevant information which is available to the coach, (iii) the complexity of the problem, (iv) the degree of cohesiveness among group members, (v) the presence or absence of time restrictions set on the decision process, (vi) the degree to which group acceptance of the decision is necessary, and (vii) the amount of power or status the coach has with regard to his or her team. Thus, Chelladurai and Haggerty (1978) actually believed that coaches should not adhere to only one decision-making style, but rather, that the particular, most effective style should vary as a function of the characteristics of the group and the situation.

Subsequent studies have shown that these seven situational factors explain a significantly greater amount of the variance in preferred and perceived decision styles than do individual differences (Chelladurai and Arnott, 1985; Chelladurai, Haggerty and Baxter, 1989; Chelladurai and Quek, 1991; Gordon, 1988). Furthermore, to assess the decision-making style used by coaches and/or the decision-making style athletes would prefer their coaches to use, these researchers developed a decision-style questionnaire that includes a number of cases, each of which describing a common sport situation with a problem to be solved. The different cases which constituted the questionnaire were chosen specifically to represent possible combinations of the abovementioned factors (e.g., low in group cohesiveness, high in problem complexity). Athletes who completed this questionnaire were requested to identify the style they believed their coaches would use in that situation or the style they would prefer their coaches to use. Coaches who completed the questionnaire were asked to identify the style they thought that they or other coaches would use in each case.

For example, Gordon (1988) administered this decision-style questionnaire to male intercollegiate football players and their respective coaches. Athletes were requested to indicate which decision style (autocratic, consultative, participative or delegative) they would prefer their coaches to use in 15 different situations and which style they believed their coaches would actually use. Coaches were requested to identify the decision style they would use in each of these 15 situations. Players also completed a coaching effectiveness questionnaire measuring their satisfaction with various aspects of their coach's behaviour. Correlational analyses of these data strongly supported the hypothesis that discrepancy between actual and preferred decision-making styles will decrease satisfaction among athletes. High ratings of the coach's effectiveness were reported when there was a high congruence between a coach's self-reported decision style and between the athletes' preferred and perceived style. It should be noted that other studies (e.g., Chelladurai and Arnott, 1985; Chelladurai, Haggerty and Baxter, 1989; Chelladurai and Quek, 1991) – using other versions of this decision-style questionnaire – did not investigate the effectiveness of coaches' decision styles; that is, these studies examined only the decision styles of coaches and/or the decision styles that athletes perceived or preferred their coaches to use, but not the effectiveness of these decision styles (see, for reviews, Chelladurai, 1993; Chelladurai and Riemer, 1998).

The Bayesian approach

In a series of investigations, Bar-Eli and his associates promoted the notion of aiding coaches' JDM processes using the Bayesian approach. The basic idea here is as follows: in some settings, the purpose of data collection is to modify the decision maker's degrees of belief in various possible hypotheses. The decision maker starts out with hypotheses about the true situation, which are often mutually exclusive and exhaustive. Even before data collection, the decision maker may believe in some of these hypotheses more strongly than in others.

However, as a result of the data, he or she may adjust his/her beliefs, some being weakened, some strengthened and others remaining unchanged. Thus, JDM can be considered as a process of alteration in a person's subjective probabilities, which are continually revised in light of accumulating data. The probabilistic relations among data and hypotheses are embodied in Reverend Thomas Bayes's theorem, which was posthumously proposed back in 1763. Psychology was introduced to Bayesian notions by Edwards (1962; see also Edwards, Lindman and Savage, 1963).

The Bayesian approach is deeply embedded within decision theory. Its basic tenets are that opinions should be expressed in terms of subjective (i.e., personal) probabilities, and that optimal revisions of such opinions in light of new relevant information should be conducted using Bayes's theorem, especially when it leads to decision making and action. Because of this concern with JDM, the output of a Bayesian analysis is often a distribution of probabilities over a set of hypothesized states of the world rather than a single prediction. These probabilities can then be used, in combination with information about payoffs associated with different states of the world and decision possibilities, to implement any of a number of decision rules. In addition, Bayes's theorem is a normative model, which specifies some internally consistent relationships among probabilistic opinions and serves also to prescribe how people should think (Rapoport and Wallsten, 1972; Slovic and Lichtenstein, 1971).

The crucial elements of the Bayesian model are conditional probabilities, which are probabilities with an 'if–then' character ('If so and so is true, then the probability of this event must be such and such'). According to Bayes's theorem, given several mutually exclusive and exhaustive hypotheses, H_i (where i is the number of hypotheses), and a datum, D (a new item of information), their relations are:

$$P(H_i/D) = \frac{P(D/H_i)\,P(H_i)}{\sum\limits_i P(D/H_i)\,P(H_i)} \qquad (6.1)$$

This formula has three basic elements: (i) Prior probability – $P(H_i)$, which represents the probability of hypothesis H_i, conditional on all information available prior to the receipt of D; (ii) Impact of new datum – $P(D/H_i)$, which is the conditional probability that datum D would be observed if hypothesis H_i is true; (iii) Posterior probability – $P(H_i/D)$, which is the probability that hypothesis H_i is true, taking into account the new datum, D, as well as all previous data.

For a set of mutually exclusive and exhaustive hypotheses H_i, the values of $P(D/H_i)$ represent the impact of the datum D on each of the hypotheses. For example, a coach may decide to try out a new test for admitting players to his or her team. In such a case, two exclusive and exhaustive hypotheses may be defined: H_1 – 'player succeeds in the team', and H_2 – 'player does not succeed in the team'. Prior to the introduction of the new test (D), the proportion $P(H_1)/P(H_2)$ had reflected the chances of each player to succeed or not in the team on the basis of all previous tests that have been conducted (therefore, the term 'prior'). After the introduction of the new test (D), the chances of each player succeeding or not are reflected by the proportion $P(H_1/D)/P(H_2/D)$, which takes into account the results of the new test, *as well as* the old ones (therefore the term 'posterior'). According to the model, it is also crucial to know the probability of a particular score in the test (D), given the fact that the player succeeded or not in the team, $P(D/H_1)/P(D/H_2)$; that is, if he or she succeeded or did not succeed in the team, which score did he or she (probably) get? This proportion reflects the impact of the new test on both hypotheses.

Equation (6.1) is appropriate for discrete hypotheses, but it can be rewritten, using integrals, to handle a continuous set of hypotheses and continuously varying data (with the denominator serving as a normalizing constant). It is often convenient to form the ratio of Equation (6.1) taken with respect to two hypotheses, H_1 and H_2, as follows:

$$\frac{P(H_1/D)}{P(H_2/D)} = \frac{P(D/H_1)}{P(D/H_2)} \cdot \frac{P(H_1)}{P(H_2)} \qquad (6.2)$$

For this ratio form, the following symbols are used:

$$\Omega_1 = LR \cdot \Omega_0 \qquad (6.3)$$

where Ω_1 represents the posterior odds, LR is the likelihood ratio, and Ω_0 stands for the prior odds.

Bayes's theorem can be applied to measure the sequential impact of several data. The posterior probability computed for the first datum is considered as the prior probability when processing the impact of the second datum and so on. Thus, the terms 'prior' and 'posterior' are relative, depending on where one is in the process of gathering information. It should be noted that the order in which data are processed makes no difference to their impact on posterior opinion, and the final posterior odds (given n items of data) are presented as:

$$\Omega n = \prod_{k-1}^{n} LR_k \cdot \Omega_o \qquad (6.4)$$

According to Equation (6.4), the data affect the final odds multiplicatively and the degree to which the prior odds are revised upon receipt of any new datum is dependent on that datum's likelihood ratio. Thus, the likelihood ratio is in fact an index of data diagnosticity (or importance, analogous to the weights employed in regression models; see Rapoport and Wallsten, 1972; Slovic and Lichtenstein, 1971). This may become clearer, for example, when one thinks about hypotheses such as 'healthy' (H_1) and 'sick' (H_2) and on a particular symptom (D) diagnosed by a medical doctor. Similarly, one could think about hypotheses (events) such as 'it will or will not rain tomorrow' (given that the weather forecast has been such as such), 'a defendant is guilty or not' (given that a particular piece of evidence has been presented to the court), or 'the national German football team will or will not win' (given that the star player Michael Ballack is in such and such shape).

Bar-Eli and his associates applied the Bayesian approach in a series of investigations on psychological performance crisis in competition (see, for review, Bar-Eli, 1997). They reasoned that in competition, athletes often experience psychological stress which may raise their arousal levels and, thereby, negatively affects their performances. Under extreme arousal levels, athletes may enter a 'psychological performance crisis', a state in which his or her ability to cope adequately with competitive requirements deteriorates substantially. Bar-Eli and Tenenbaum (1989a) maintained that a crisis state develops when a system (athlete) is no longer characterized by stability (Phase A), but is progressively over- or undercharged and, thus, may be characterized by an increasing lability (Phase B). In the case of extreme lability, failure of coping and defence mechanisms may lead to crisis (Phase C). If one defines events C ('crisis') and $\bar{C}$ ('no crisis') as mutually exclusive and exhaustive, then $P(C) + P(\bar{C}) = 1$. In Phase A, $P(C) \ll P(\bar{C})$; in Phase B, $P(C) < P(\bar{C})$ or $P(C) \approx P(\bar{C})$ or $P(C) > P(\bar{C})$, and in Phase C, $P(C) \gg P(\bar{C})$; the probabilities of all these phases sum up to 1.

From this model (for a detailed explanation, see Bar-Eli and Tenenbaum, 1989a) a formal diagnosis framework was derived, with reference to the development of an athlete's psychological performance crisis in competition. The probabilistic measure of diagnostic value used for this purpose was based on the Bayesian approach which had previously been applied in expert systems, for example, in order to help geologists look for mineral deposits (Duda *et al.*, 1976), or to provide probabilities for medical diagnosis (Eddy, 1982; Schwartz, Baron and Clarke, 1988). The use of the Bayesian approach for diagnostic purposes rests on the assumption that, quite often, decision makers do have substantial difficulties in weighing and combining (i.e., aggregating) information as a result of their limited information-processing and decision-making capabilities (Tenenbaum and Bar-Eli, 1993). Accordingly, JDM should be decomposed into a number of presumably simpler estimation tasks, in an attempt to circumvent aggregation difficulties by having people estimate separate components and letting a computer system combine them. Hence, when a total problem is fractionated into a series of structurally related parts and experts are asked to assess these fractions, JDM processes can be substantially aided (Armstrong, Denniston and Gordon, 1975; Gettys *et al.*, 1973). In case of only two hypotheses, H_1 and H_2, people estimate $P(D/H_1)$ and $P(D/H_2)$ values, which are integrated across hypotheses and across data through Bayes's theorem (see Equation (6.2)). After all the relevant data have been processed, the resulting output is a ratio of posterior probabilities, $P(H_1/D)/P(H_2/D)$. In this way, a probabilistic diagnosis may be improved significantly (Edwards, 1962; Slovic, Fischhoff and Lichtenstein, 1977; Slovic and Lichtenstein, 1971). It is no wonder, then, that the use of these principles for diagnostic purposes has been repeatedly recommended within various contexts which involve JDM processes (Baron, 2008).

As mentioned above, Bar-Eli and his associates investigated these ideas, thereby introducing the use of the Bayesian approach to sport psychology through applying it to the crisis model (see Bar-Eli, 1984). H_1 and H_2 in Equation (6.2) were replaced by the two following mutually exclusive and exhaustive hypotheses: (i) (C) – The athlete is in a psychological performance crisis during the competition; (ii) ($\bar{C}$) – The athlete is not in a psychological performance crisis during the competition. As a result, Equation (6.2) took the form of:

$$\frac{P(C/D)}{P(\bar{C}/D)} = \frac{P(D/C)}{P(D/\bar{C})} \cdot \frac{P(C)}{P(\bar{C})} \qquad (6.5)$$

The diagnosis of crisis required, that diagnostic factors be identified. Through these factors, the problem of diagnosing an athlete's psychological performance crisis in competition could be fractionated. Each such factor included several components (i.e., Bayesian data), which could be separately assessed by experts with regard to their probability of occurrence when a crisis [P(D/C)] or a non-crisis [P(D/$\bar{C}$)] occurs. Later on, the ratio of $P(C/D)/P(\bar{C}/D)$ could be computed by Bayes's rule. These factors included pre-start susceptibility to crisis, time-phases, perceived team performance, performance quality and behavioural violations and crisis related social factors such as teammates, coach, spectators and referees, which were investigated using both subjective and observational research methods (see, for review, Bar-Eli, 1997).

At this point the Bayesian model, as presented in Equation (6.5), could be used to aid coaches' JDM regarding athletes' psychological states in competition as follows: upon exposure to information about the existence of a particular datum (i.e., a component of one of the diagnostic factors), the ratio of probabilities concerning the occurrence of the two events, C and $\bar{C}$, could be revised, all previous data being taken into account. For this purpose, however, the technical hurdle of computerizing such a diagnosis process had to be overcome. Furthermore, in order for the entire process to be effective, posterior probabilities had to be associated with practical measures aimed at coping with players' psycho-regulative problems at each phase of crisis development during competition, as outlined in more detail by Bar-Eli and Tenenbaum (1989a).

Heuristics/biases and creativity: Implications for (successful) coaching

As mentioned previously, Bar-Eli and his associates initiated a series of studies on heuristics and biases (Azar and Bar-Eli, 2008; Bar-Eli, Avugos *et al.*, 2006; Bar-Eli and Azar, 2009; Bar-Eli *et al.*, 2007) and creativity (Bar-Eli, Lowengart *et al.*, 2006; Bar-Eli, Lowengart *et al.*, 2008; Goldenberg *et al.*, 2004; Goldenberg *et al.*, 2010) in sport. Although they did not directly investigate coaches' behaviour, these studies may have some significant implications for successful coaching.

Bar-Eli, Avugos *et al.* (2006) reviewed the literature on the 'hot hand' phenomenon in which they included both the empirical research based on real data and statistical examinations of simulated data. The authors concluded that, although the issue has been extensively discussed in the literature, the question of whether success breeds success and failure breeds failure remains unresolved. According to this review, most of the empirical research supports Gilovich, Vallone and Tversky's (1985) argument concerning the non-existence of a relationship between future success and past performance (the sequential dependence claim). This has been strongly evident in professional basketball as well as in a few other sports. However, simulation studies demonstrate that fluctuations in success rates are present (the non-stationarity claim) and that the conventional tests in use are often unable to detect them. The implications for (successful) coaching are almost self-evident, because, if streak hitters or shooters do in fact exist, future research should then identify the conditions in which they may emerge and the coaching methods should be adapted and improved accordingly. However, if athletic performance is unconditionally not elevated due to past success, obviously the coaching and/or mental techniques commonly used in both training and competitions should be substantially reconsidered.

Bar-Eli, Lowengart *et al.* (2006) investigated a well-known example of creativity in sport, namely, the case of the elite high jumper Dick Fosbury. In the 1968 Mexico Olympics, Fosbury – instead of trying to excel in the high jump by utilizing established means – broke with tradition and invented a radically new approach to the high jump, later dubbed the 'Fosbury Flop'. A theoretical analysis of this case conducted by these authors using an extensively detailed introspective report, provided by Fosbury himself, demonstrated that this radical innovation was not an outcome of 'total freedom' of thought (as would have been argued, for example, by authors such as Csikszentmihalyi, 1996), but rather the outcome of a continuous development process and a combination of converging abilities.

Several lessons may be drawn from a close examination of the Fosbury case (see also Goldenberg *et al.*, 2004; Goldenberg *et al.*, 2010). For example, Fosbury reported that the incremental development of the new style was a spontaneous reaction during competition. In other words, the fact that he was highly intense and focused during competition, did not make him stick to a well-learned behaviour or habit – as would be predicted from classical learning theories such as the Hull–Spence model for instance (e.g., Spence and Spence, 1966) – but rather led him to seek changes and innovations. Moreover, it is evident from Fosbury's case that experts' optimal (i.e., normative) solutions to various problems investigated in the expert sport performance literature (Starkes and Ericsson, 2003) can frequently be a matter of a transient consensus and/or sheer ignorance.

Bar-Eli, Lowengart *et al.* (2006) recommended that methods such as the paradoxical approach (Bar-Eli, 1991) are to be used to promote 'irrationality' in sport. However, taking a closer look into creativity in sport, it can be concluded that, in order to develop peak performers, the principles of optimization and creativity-enhancement should not be considered controversial; they should rather be integrated through a complementary implementation. These recommendations were further strengthened by Bar-Eli, Lowengart *et al.*'s (2008) study in which a comparative analysis was conducted between two great inventions – Tsukahara's Vault and Fosbury's Flop. The comparison between these two cases revealed an amazingly similar pattern in the structure of the innovative process. The major conclusion drawn from this analysis is – again – that, in order to promote innovative processes in sport, the principles of optimization and creativity-enhancement should be applied complimentarily.

A general implication for successful coaching to be derived from these studies on heuristics/biases and creativity in sport would be that athletes' cognitions should be systematically trained. According to Vickers (2007), common training practices are usually intended to change athletes' behaviour, but they have mainly short-term effects. In order to achieve long-term, consistent and reliable performance improvements, coaches are advised to put a stronger emphasis on training athletes' cognitive skills required for high-level performances. To promote such skills in athletes, Vickers herself suggested that coaches should be taught to design decision-training practices which could help athletes learn to anticipate events better on court, as well as to focus and attend to critical cues in order to become effective decision makers under stressful, competitive conditions in the field.

The decision-training programme suggested by Vickers (available and tested since 1994; see Vickers, 2007, for review) includes three steps, seven cognitive skills, seven cognitive triggers and seven decision-training tools. In the first step, a decision to be trained is identified, highlighting one of seven cognitive skills (anticipation, attention, focus and concentration, pattern recognition, memory, problem solving, decision making). In the second step, a drill is designed and trained in a realistic setting using a cognitive trigger (that is, one of the following seven cues: object, location, quiet-eye, reaction time, memory retrieval, kinaesthetic, self-coaching). In the third step, one or more of seven decision-training tools (i.e., variable or random practice, bandwidth, video feedback, questioning, hard-first instruction, modelling, external focus of instruction) is selected in order to train the decision in a variety of contexts.

The effectiveness of this decision-training programme was recently demonstrated with athletes in baseball (Vickers *et al.*, 1999), table tennis (Raab, Masters and Maxwell, 2005) and swimming (Chambers and Vickers, 2006). It remains to be seen whether the application of this programme to improve coaches' own decisions, will indeed lead these (trained) coaches to become better decision makers on court. Although this particular question was not investigated thus far, Vickers *et al.* (2004) maintained that the continued use of decision-training methods, after first being introduced to the programme, had a positive effect on coaches' future employment and success. These findings could probably encourage coaches to use such decision-training methods to promote not only their athletes' JDM, but also their own.

SUMMARY

Managers and coaches are usually considered as leaders; therefore, JDM can be conceived as a major leadership task. We presented first processes associated with managerial JDM. We discussed decision –types and –environments, reviewed some major decision-making models, and considered different processes related to group and organizational decisions. Later on, we focused on coaches' JDM. We discussed the concept of decision styles, the Bayesian approach, and the implications of the heuristics/biases paradigm and the updated research on creativity in sport for successful coaching. The current state of the art in these areas was reviewed, including discussion of future trends and perspectives in light of possible obstacles and limitations.

Referees

7

Referees

An ideal of sport competitions is expressed in the traditional notion:
'May the best man win'. In order to increase the chances that the best
athlete or team indeed wins a competition, referees (sometimes called
umpires, officials, linesmen or judges) are installed in almost all
competitive sports in order to ensure the course of a competition in
accordance with the rules of the respective sport. Of course, their tasks
and their possible influence on the outcome of a competition differ
between sports. For example, in gymnastics the assessment of athletes'
performance exclusively depends on human judgement while in track
and fields they are supposed to be measured objectively. Accordingly,
Stefani (1998) differentiates between three ways in which performance
is evaluated in sports, that is, if the outcome of a sport competition
is assessed by an objective measurement (e.g., time in swimming), an
objective score (e.g., goals in football), or a subjective judgement
(e.g., points in figure skating). Almost a third of all sports that are
recognized by the International Olympic Committee (IOC) are considered to have a performance rating system in which judging plays a
major role. But even when sport performance is assessed in an objective
way, there is often a judgement of referees involved beyond these
objective values. For example, in an ambiguous tackling situation, a
football referee has to decide whether to award a penalty or a linesman

Judgement, Decision Making and Success in Sport, First Edition.
M. Bar-Eli, H. Plessner and M. Raab.
© 2011 John Wiley & Sons, Ltd. Published 2011 by John Wiley & Sons, Ltd.

in tennis who has no 'hawk eye' available needs to decide whether a ball was on the line or just out.

This chapter presents research on the processes that underlie referee's judgements and decisions, while following the steps of social information processing from perception to information integration (see Chapter 2, Social cognition). Not surprisingly, most of the present research on referee decisions is concerned with potential biases and errors. After all, referees receive public attention for (obvious) decision errors rather than for their extraordinary skills and achievements. Thus, the practical idea behind most research with a focus on referee's biases and errors is, that revealing their underlying processes is a first step in order to improve referee's decision making. However, this requires an understanding of referee's tasks at first.

THE TASKS OF REFEREES

In order to compare the tasks and demands of referees across different sports, MacMahon and Plessner (2008) propose some general categories: interactors, monitors and reactors. These categories are based on two dimensions: the amount of interaction with athletes on the playing/ competition surface and the number of athletes or cues that are being monitored (see Figure 7.1).

Among others, this categorization of referees determines the relative importance of different research questions, findings and thus training. For example, while physical fitness is of highest importance as a prerequisite for decision making of a typical interactor, such as a football referee (Helsen and Bultynck, 2004; Mascarenhas, O'Hare and Plessner, 2006), this is of minor importance for a typical monitor such as a gymnastic judge, to whom perceptual-cognitive skills become increasingly emphasized (Salmela, 1978). In addition, the more referees are supposed to interact with athletes the more important becomes personality and management. This has also an impact on what can be considered as a *good* decision.

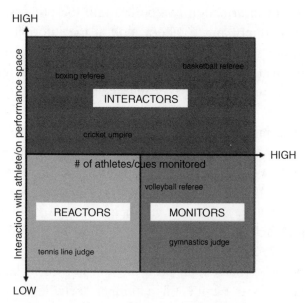

Figure 7.1 A classification system for sport officials (MacMahon and Plessner, 2008).

Theoretical as well as recent empirical research suggests that the decisions of sport game referees can be motivated by either of the two goals: *enforcement of the laws of the game*, that is, to be accurate (Plessner and Betsch, 2002), or *game management*, that is, to ensure the flow of the game, to be/appear unbiased (Mascarenhas, Collins and Mortimer, 2002; Rains, 1984). While these goals mostly point in the same direction, they can also get into conflict in certain decision situations (Brand, Schweizer and Plessner, 2009). Hence, while most of the research in this field is concerned with accurate decision making, one should also keep in mind that referees are also expected to adjust their interpretation of incidents to the concrete context of the situation in question in many sports.

PERCEPTUAL LIMITATIONS

If a judgement of performance is intended to mirror the *true* performance of an athlete, performance must first be perceived accurately, so that the relevant information can be fed into the processing system. Therefore, it is important to take a look at the information a judge attends to before he or she evaluates a performance or makes decisions about rule applications. Ideally, all stimuli that are relevant for judging a performance are processed. But because the human capacity to process information is limited, a judge needs to select, which stimuli should undergo further processing. At best, judges know how to allocate their attention. For instance, expert judges in gymnastics have been shown to differ from novices in their visual search strategies (Bard *et al.*, 1980). By and large, this research shows that expert judges in sports develop effective anticipatory strategies that help to improve their decision making (e.g., MacMahon and Ste-Marie, 2002; Mather, 2008; Paull and Glencross, 1997; Ste-Marie, 1999, 2000).

The influence of perceptual processes on judgement and decision making in sports is also evident in a number of studies concerning the visual perspective from which the athlete's behaviour is observed. It is therefore important to understand if expert judges in sport are aware of the potential biasing influence of their viewing position and are able to control it. The results of studies on this issue provide a rather pessimistic answer. For example, Oudejans *et al.* (2000) found that the high percentage of assistant referees' errors in offside decisions in football mainly reflects their viewing position. Although they should stand in line with the last defender, on average they are positioned too far behind. By considering the retinal images of referees, Oudejans *et al.* (2000) predicted a specific relation of frequencies in different types of errors (flag error: wrongly indicating offside vs. non-flag error: not indicating an actual offside) depending on the area of attack (near vs. far from the assistant referee and inside or outside the defender). In an analysis of several videotaped matches this prediction was confirmed, thus, demonstrating that assistant referees' decisions directly reflect the situations as they are projected on their retinas. In a follow-up study Oudejans *et al.* (2005) replicated their findings by analysing special video recordings with 215 potential offside situations from four matches of one team in the Dutch Eredivisie. Comparable to the results of their previous study, assistant referees were exactly in line with the second last defender in only 13.5% of the potential offside situations. Typically, they were positioned about 1 metre away from this ideal position. Furthermore, there was a relationship between the speed that the assistant referees were moving and the numbers of errors: there were more errors when the assistant referees were running or sprinting than when they were walking or jogging. This corresponds well to the authors' essential idea: one of the most challenging tasks of assistant referees in football is that they have to 'fight for' an exact position on the actual offside line in order to judge offside situations correctly.

Another explanation for the high frequency of errors in offside decisions that has been proposed is the flash-lag effect, contributed by Baldo, Ranvaud and Morya (2002). The authors introduce their approach as an attempt to apply to a real life situation a perceptual phenomenon that has been studied in laboratory setups for many years. The flash-lag effect is where 'a moving object is perceived as spatially leading its real position at an instant defined by a time marker' (Baldo, Ranvaud and Morya, 2002, p. 1205). Based on laboratory research, the perceptual advancement caused by the flash-lag effect is estimated as being 0.02 and 0.64 metres. This means that assistant referees perceive the receiving player as being this distance ahead of his actual position.

Baldo, Ranvaud and Morya (2002) propose the flash-lag effect to be responsible for an overall bias they discovered in Oudejans *et al.*'s (2000) data, namely that assistant referees generally seem to commit more flag errors (57%) than non-flag errors (43%). Baldo, Ranvaud and Morya's (2002) idea is that an assistant referee's positioning ahead of the actual offside line in combination with the predictions of the flash-lag effect leads to an enlarged area susceptible to flag errors on left trajectories, and a much smaller area susceptible for non-flag errors on right trajectories.

The introduction of the flash-lag hypothesis to this topic has triggered an interesting debate about which theory comes off best. Helsen, Gilis and Weston (2006, p. 527) contend that their data 'clearly support' the flash-lag hypothesis. In contrast Oudejans, Bakker and Beek (2007) state that this conclusion is based on misinterpretations and that Helsen, Gilis and Weston's (2006) dataset is not suited to test the optical error hypothesis. Thus, further research is necessary to disentangle the two hypotheses (relevant proposals have been described by Mascarenhas, O'Hare and Plessner, 2006). Hopefully, it will show which one of the two hypotheses – or the combination of both, as proposed by Baldo, Ranvaud and Morya (2002) – will prove to be more successful in explaining erroneous offside judgements in football assistant referees.

In a similar vein as Oudejans *et al.* (2005), Plessner and Schallies (2005) examined the influence of judges' viewing position on the evaluation of exercise presentation in men's gymnastics. This is also of practical interest because the position from where judges have to evaluate exercises is only loosely prescribed in the rules of gymnastics. In an experiment, experienced gymnastic judges and laypeople were presented with a series of photographs, which show athletes holding a cross on rings. They were simultaneously taken from different viewpoints (0, 30 or 60 degrees from frontal view). Participants had to judge how many degrees the arms deviated from horizontal for each picture. This is a natural judgement task for gymnastic judges prescribed by the rules. It has been expected to be more difficult, the more the viewpoint differs from frontal view. Half of the group of judges had the secondary task to judge the duration of the picture presentation, which also varied. This again resembled a task that judges have to fulfil under natural conditions. It was found that the overall performance of the referees was much better than that of the laypeople. In contrast to the lay judgements, they were not influenced by the secondary task. However, the expert judgement was still significantly influenced by the viewing position – meaning, the error rate increased with an increase in deviation from a frontal view. Although expertise led to more accurate judgements and helped to overcome capacity limitations, it did not prevent judges from being influenced by basic perceptual limitations (see also Ford *et al.*, 1997; Ford, Goodwin and Richardson, 1995).

In accordance with these results and those of other studies (e.g., Bard *et al.*, 1980; MacMahon and Ste-Marie, 2002; Ste-Marie, 1999, 2000), Ste-Marie (2003b) drew this conclusion: if judgements of experienced referees in some sports are indeed found to be more accurate than the judgement of lay people or novices, it is because experienced referees in general do not encounter the same processing limitations as novices. Based on a problem-solving approach, she argued that experienced referees have some specific knowledge that helps them with processing capacities. They know what information is relevant, what to expect and what are the typical interrelations among variables. This may be of even more concern in the sports domain than in other areas of expertise research because sport evaluation occurs under time-pressured situations with continuously incoming information. This kind of knowledge seems not to be attained as an automatic consequence of mere experience in a sport – for example, as an athlete (Allard *et al.*, 1993) – but it would also need some specific, structured and effortful training at best. In accordance with this reasoning, recent research supports the notion that refereeing performance is highly dependent on levels of expertise. FIFA referees are better in making decisions for football incidents than national referees and national referees again are better than players (Gilis *et al.*, 2006; Gilis *et al.*, 2008; MacMahon *et al.*, 2007).

However, beyond perceptual aspects of information processing there may be other basic processes that influence referees before any conscious processes and decision skills come into play (Brand, Plessner and Unkelbach, 2008). For example, Unkelbach and Memmert (2008) draw on classic psychophysical models of categorization in order to explain the fact that referees in football games do not award as many yellow cards in the beginning of a game as should be statistically expected. Based on the consistency model by Haubensak (1992) they argue that the effect is a necessity of the judgement situation: referees need to calibrate a judgement scale, and, to preserve degrees of freedom in that scale, they need to avoid extreme category judgements in the beginning (i.e., yellow cards). In a series of experiments and analyses of field data, they found support for these assumptions.

The examples presented in this section demonstrate how error rates and distribution patterns over time can be explained by basic psychological principles. That does not mean, however, that referees' decision errors cannot emerge during later steps of information processing and from motivated or strategic thinking. It is of course plausible to assume that these later processes will sometimes add to the size of the reported errors and frequently produce errors of their own, as we will see soon. Nevertheless, basic psychological processes need to be studied in this domain in order to understand the baseline on which higher inference processes may operate. For example, if a referee's perceived information is already sufficiently biased it is hardly surprising to find his or her final decision to be false. In this case one needs not to assume additional bias during later steps of information processing.

PRIOR KNOWLEDGE

Once information about an athlete's performance is perceived, a judge encodes and interprets the information by giving it meaning. In order to encode and categorize new information, it must be related to prior knowledge stored in memory. For example, a floor routine in gymnastics may appear as a random sequence of strange movements to an inexperienced observer, unlike a gymnastic expert, who will easily be able to recognize several categories of elements that differ in difficulty. While prior knowledge about judgement criteria in a sport and adequate categorization systems are necessary requirements for accurate performance judgements (MacMahon and Ste-Marie, 2002; Paull and Glencross, 1997; Ste-Marie, 1999, 2000), we focus our overview on research about the use of inappropriate knowledge – that is, knowledge that has a distorting or biasing influence on judges' cognitive processes and subsequent decisions (cf. Plessner, 2005).

Frank and Gilovich (1988) were able to show that culturally shared, seemingly irrelevant knowledge for a judgement of a performance can have an influence on sport decisions. They assumed that in most cultures, there is a strong association between the colour black and aggression. The black uniform of a sports team, therefore, could serve as a prime that automatically activates the concept of aggression, thus, increasing its accessibility. In two studies and one experiment, evidence was found that players perceived themselves as more aggressive and behaved accordingly, when they were dressed in black as opposed to other colours. In an additional experiment, Frank and

Gilovich (1988) found that American football referees were more likely to penalize a team wearing a black uniform than a team wearing a white uniform. Still, this effect seems not to be valid for all cultures. In a study with Turkish football referees, Tiryaki (2005) found no comparable influence of black uniforms. In a more recent study, Hagemann, Strauss and Leißing (2008) found that tae kwon do competitors were favoured by the referees when they wore red instead of blue protective gear. In an experiment, they asked experienced referees to indicate how many points they would award red and blue competitors who were presented in videotaped excerpts from sparring rounds. The video clips were manipulated in a way that for half of the presentations the colours of the competitors were reversed technically. The results showed that the competitor wearing red protective gear was awarded on average more points than the competitor wearing blue protective gear (see Figure 7.2). This could at least partly explain the more general finding by Hill and Barton (2005) who showed that wearing red sports attire has a positive impact on one's outcome in a combat sport.

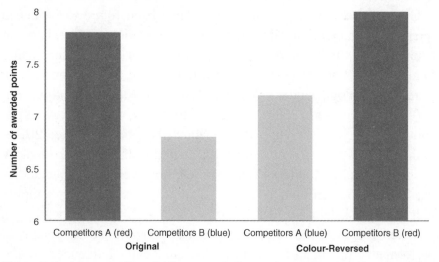

Figure 7.2 Mean number of points awarded to tae kwon do competitors in original and colour-reversed versions of videotaped fights (Hagemann, Strauss and Leißing, 2008).

The encoding of information about sport performances has also been found to be influenced by categories that evolve directly from the competitive environment. For example in gymnastics, the fact that gymnastics coaches typically place their gymnasts in rank order from poorest at the beginning to best at the end in a team competition, leads to different performance expectancies. These expectancies have been found to exert a biasing influence on the evaluation of exercises in gymnastics (Ansorge *et al.*, 1978; Scheer, 1973; Scheer and Ansorge, 1975, 1979), figure skating (Bruine de Bruin, 2005, 2006) and synchronized swimming (Wilson, 1977). In an experiment following this line of research, Plessner (1999) investigated the cognitive processes underlying expectancy effects in gymnastics judging. Gymnastic judges were asked to score videotaped routines of a men's team competition. The target routines appeared in either the first or the fifth position of within-team order. Dependent on the difficulty of the judgement task, a significant effect of placement was found: the same routine received lower scores when placed in the first position than placed in the last position. Additionally, it was found that the categorization of perceived value parts (i.e., the attributed difficulty to single gymnastic elements) were biased by judges' expectancies.

Other sources of expectancies that have been found to influence referees' judgements and decisions are the reputation of an athlete or a team (Findlay and Ste-Marie, 2004; Jones, Paull and Erskine, 2002; Lehman and Reifman, 1987; Rainey, Larsen and Stephenson, 1989), stereotypes about gender (Coulomb-Cabagno, Rascle and Souchon, 2005; Souchon *et al.*, 2004) and race (Stone, Perry and Darley, 1997) and even players' height (Van Quaquebeke and Giessner, 2010). Although these influences have been treated in the literature mainly as unwelcome, it should be remembered, however, that expectancies that mirror true differences can also improve accuracy in complex judgement tasks (Jussim, 1991).

Taken together, the encoding and categorization of a perceived performance has been found to be systematically influenced by the activation of various types of prior knowledge, even when this knowledge has no performance-relevant value in judging an athlete's performance. It is clear that these influences increase in likelihood as judging situations increase in ambiguity. However, such situations seem to occur quite often in sport competitions. For example, Nevill, Balmer and Williams (2002) asked referees to make assessments for 47 typical incidents taken from an English Premier League match. One of the findings was that none of these challenges resulted in a unanimous decision by all qualified referees participating in the study (see also Teipel, Gerisch and Busse, 1983).

While the studies reported so far demonstrate that judgements of performance are potentially biased by the activation of general memory structures, there is also some evidence for direct memory influences on the judgement of sport performances. Such influences have been studied in an impressive series of experiments by Ste-Marie and her colleagues (Ste-Marie, 2003a; Ste-Marie and Lee, 1991; Ste-Marie and Valiquette, 1996; Ste-Marie, Valiquette and Taylor, 2001). They investigated how the memory of prior encounters with an athlete's performance can influence actual performance judgements. In these experiments, a paradigm was developed that mirrors the warm-up/competition setting in gymnastics. In the first phase of the experiment, judges watched a series of gymnasts perform a simple element and decided whether the performance was perfect or flawed. The judges' task was the same in the second phase that followed, except that the gymnastic elements shared a relationship with the items shown in the first phase. Some of the gymnasts were shown during the second phase with the identical performance as in the first phase (e.g., both times perfect), and others were shown with the opposite performance (e.g., first perfect and then flawed). When the performance in the first and second phases differed, perceptual judgements were less accurate than when performances were the same for both phases (Ste-Marie and Lee, 1991). These memory-influenced biases occurred even with a week break between the first and second phases (Ste-Marie and Valiquette, 1996) and irrespective of the cognitive task that the judges had to perform during the first phase (Ste-Marie, 2003a). The robustness of this effect supports the authors' assumption that perceptual judgements, such as in judging gymnastics, inevitably rely on retrieval from memory for prior episodes. Thus, the only way to avoid these biases would be to prevent judges from seeing the gymnasts perform before a competition (Ste-Marie and Lee, 1991).

RULES OF INFORMATION INTEGRATION

In the final step of social information processing, information about an athlete's performance that has been encoded and categorized together with information that has been retrieved from memory, are integrated into a judgement. Ideally, a judge considers all the relevant information for a judgement task at hand and integrates this information in the most appropriate, analytical way. But because the human capacities to process information are limited and social situations often introduce constraints such as time pressure, people frequently use shortcuts to cope with complex judgement situations (see Chapter 2, Social cognition). An example for these mentioned shortcuts is the availability heuristic (see Chapter 8, Biases in judgements of sport performance) or the use of schematic knowledge, which is classified as top-down processing (e.g., Fiske and Neuberg, 1990). Unfortunately, little is known about when and why judges in sport switch between bottom-up and top-down processing. Research on information integration processes in sport performance judgements typically focuses on the more or less deliberate use of information beyond the observable performance.

Nevill, Balmer and Williams (1999, 2002) investigated whether crowd noise has an influence on football referees' decisions concerning potential foul situations. They assumed that referees have learned to use crowd noise as a decision cue because in general it may serve as a useful indicator for the seriousness of the foul. But, the use of this knowledge may be inappropriate and may contribute to the well-confirmed phenomenon of a home advantage in team sports, because the reaction of a crowd is usually biased against the away team (Courneya and Carron, 1992). In an experiment, referees assessed various challenges videotaped from a match in the English Premier League. Half of the referees observed the video with the original crowd noise audible, whereas the other half viewed the video in silence. This presence or absence of crowd noise had an effect on decisions made by the referees. Most importantly, referees who viewed challenges in the noise condition awarded significantly fewer fouls against the home team than those observing the video in silence. The authors concluded that this effect might be partly due to heuristic judgement processes in which the salient, yet potentially biased, judgement of the crowd served as a decision cue for referees. In a recent series of studies Unkelbach and Memmert (2010) presented convincing evidence for this assumption. Among others, these studies demonstrate how biased referees decisions can contribute to the phenomenon of a home advantage in sports (see also Balmer, Nevill and Lane, 2005; Boyko, Boyko and Boyko, 2007; Sutter and Kocher, 2004).

Some other studies show that referees are not only influenced by situational cues but by their own prior decisions (e.g., Damisch, Mussweiler and Plessner, 2006; MacMahon and Starkes, 2008; Plessner and Betsch, 2001). In an experimental study, Plessner and Betsch (2001) found a negative contingency between football referees' successive penalty decisions concerning the same team. This means that the probability of awarding a penalty to a team decreased when they had awarded a penalty to this team in a similar situation before and increased when they had not. The opposite effect occurred with successive penalty decisions concerning the first one and then the other team. Similar results have been found with basketball referees when contact situations were presented in their original game sequence but not when they were presented as random successions of individual scenes (Brand, Schmidt and Schneeloch, 2006). In an impressive analysis of field data from about 13,000 football matches, Schwarz (2011) presented further evidence for corresponding compensating tendencies in penalty kick decisions of referees. Among others, he could show that the number of two-penalty matches is larger than expected by chance, and that among these matches there are considerably more matches in which each team is awarded one penalty than would be expected on the basis of independent penalty kick decisions. Additional analyses based on the score in the match before a penalty is awarded and on the timing of penalties suggest that awarding a first penalty to one team raises the referee's penalty evidence criterion for the same team, and lowers the corresponding criterion for the other team. Together, these effects may be partly due to referees' goal of being fair in the management of a game (Mascarenhas, Collins and Mortimer, 2002; Rains, 1984).

Sequential effects also point to the fact that social judgements are comparative in nature (Mussweiler, 2003). The judgement of an athlete's performance is frequently based on the comparison with other athletes or with prior judgements of other athletes' performance respectively. Recent research suggests that the consequences of such comparisons are produced by the selective accessibility mechanism of similarity and dissimilarity testing (Mussweiler, 2003). That means, starting the comparison process with the focus on similarities increases the likelihood of an assimilation judgement towards the standard of comparison. The focus on dissimilarities, however, is more likely to end up in a contrast effect away from a standard. These assumptions were recently applied to the sequential judgement of gymnastic routines on vault by experienced judges (Damisch, Mussweiler and Plessner, 2006). Two athletes were introduced to the judges as belonging either to the same national team (similarity focus) or to different teams (dissimilarity focus). The routines of both gymnasts had to be evaluated in a sequence. While the second routine was the same in all conditions, half of the participants first saw a better routine (high standard), while the other half first saw a worse routine (low standard). As predicted, the second gymnast's score was assimilated towards the standard when both gymnasts were introduced as belonging to the same team. The opposite effect occurred when the judges believed the gymnasts belonged to different teams (see Figure 7.3).

While most of the reported biases are due to the functioning of the cognitive information processing system so far, it is clear that many biases in judgements or sport performance also have a motivational background. Starting with the work by Hastorf and Cantril (1954), there

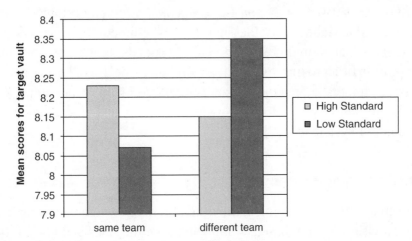

Figure 7.3 Mean scores for a routine that followed either a better or a weaker performance when judges either believed that the two gymnasts belong to the same team or to different teams (Damisch, Mussweiler and Plessner, 2006).

is plenty of evidence that group membership has a distorting influence on the judgement of sport performances (Ansorge and Scheer, 1988; de Fiore and Kramer, 1982; Markman and Hirt, 2002; Mohr and Larsen, 1998; Seltzer and Glass, 1991; Ste-Marie, 1996; Whissell *et al.*, 1993). Thus, achieving accuracy is not the only motivation that should be taken into account when studying biases in the judgement of sport performance. To conform to a norm may be just another goal (Rainey and Larsen, 1988; Rainey *et al.*, 1993; Scheer, Ansorge and Howard, 1983; Van den Auweele *et al.*, 2004; Wanderer, 1987). Only one study has until now directly assessed whether influences like these are automatic or unconscious (Ste-Marie, 1996). However, no support was found for the hypothesis of unconscious influences.

IMPROVING REFEREES' JDM

As said in the beginning of this chapter, the demands and skills vary a great deal between different types of officials, from the smaller differences between the referee and assistant referee to the bigger differences between a gymnastics judge and a football referee. None-theless, MacMahon and Plessner (2008) pointed to some general principles that should be considered by officials, judges, referees and umpires in order to improve their performance: the use of basic training systems, understanding the demands of refereeing, identification of key decisions and typical errors, advance training and development of evaluation systems.

Basic training systems

The most basic requirement in officiating, on which licensing and accreditation is often based, is knowledge of the rules and laws of the sport. Hence, referees are required to have a strong foundation of declarative knowledge, which is often defined as rulebook knowledge. The implementation of the rules is referred to as procedural (how to) knowledge. For learning of the rules and learning of rule application, most sports provide material in the form of commentaries and accompanying videos helping the novice official to become familiar with the specific rule system beyond the mere study of the written rules. For example, a corresponding training tool has been developed on a sound theoretical basis for football referees' foul decisions (Brand, Schweizer and Plessner, 2009; Plessner *et al.*, 2009; Schweizer, Plessner and Brand, 2010). Among others, the tool was developed to meet the requirements of a general learning approach to intuition (Plessner, Betsch and Betsch, 2008). Three key assumptions guided the tool's development. In order to improve their intuitive decision making, referees need to benefit from kind feedback structures in representative environments over extensive periods of time. The training tool is web-based and consists of a database and an online training module. Stored in the database are numerous video sequences. These sequences are rather short (about 10 seconds) and show possible foul situations, that is, a contact between two or more players. They were selected from recordings of soccer matches from different soccer leagues. For each video-item the German Soccer Association's referee board has provided the normatively correct decision. Referees participating in the training programme get access to an online platform. Via this platform they attend regular training sessions. During each session they are shown several video-items of possible foul situations. Video-items are stopped immediately after the contact to be judged. Referees are asked to indicate their decision via mouse-click on respective buttons. They have to choose between the options no foul and foul. In the case of the latter decision, they are subsequently asked to indicate the appropriate sanction (free kick, yellow card, red card). Immediately after having indicated their decision, referees receive feedback on the correctness of their decision. Feedback is generated via an online comparison between the referee's decision and the correct decision as stored in the database. For all decisions, referees can be set under time pressure. First evaluation studies support the effectiveness of this procedure (Schweizer *et al.*, 2011).

Such training tools are also important because laws are typically written with the main purpose of being exact and not of being user-friendly. In addition, in some sports learning the rules is already the greatest challenge for the future official. For example, the code of points in gymnastics is rather complex and comprises, among other things, a detailed list of hundreds of value parts that need to be recognized in a competition. Again, it seems that this kind of knowledge is not attained as an automatic consequence of mere experience in a sport – for example as an athlete – but it is acquired through specific, structured and effortful training. Apart from video material, that can be helpful in order to learn both the rules and how to implement them, officials are also advised to observe and discuss athletes' performances frequently, either in training sessions or competitions.

Understanding the demands of refereeing

Officials are often left out in the cold in terms of a research basis for their training. They are left to rely on what is known about training for the athletes in their sport. This is not entirely inappropriate for some skills. For example, the fitness and physical training of the football official should be somewhat similar to that of the football athlete. However, there are also specific demands on the official, keeping in mind that some of these are additional and/or different to those of the athlete. These demands may differ depending on the level of play that is officiated and the gender of the athletes. Demands may be assessed by watching a selection of videotaped performances and by coding the action using a number of categories:

- Movement patterns (e.g., forward, sideways, backwards; sprinting, jogging, walking)
- Communication (e.g., length, number of communications with other officials, athletes, coaches)
- Number and type of decisions

Identification of the key decisions and typical errors

Once the demands are understood, they can be used to identify key decisions, typical areas of difficulty and even sources of error. As has been shown in prior sections, the social information processing approach is helpful to identify the stage at which errors have occurred. Thus, positioning may be a large source of perceptual difficulty, for example, which leads to error in a particular decision. Once again, key decisions may differ by level of play and undoubtedly for different types of decision-making systems (e.g., panel of judges versus on-field referee). This type of analysis can provide information on common practices, types of systems and their influences on decision making, for example, the use of a panel of judges responsible for providing a global mark for an athlete versus split responsibilities (e.g., technical and artistic assessments as in gymnastics).

Advanced training

The next obvious step is to use the information gained from an assessment of demands and errors to guide training. In physically demanding officiating, training should build an aerobic base and mimic the on-field demands. The training literature provides a great deal more specific guidance here. Concerning decisions, officials can now become sensitized to which key decisions require additional focus in video tools, the law book and positioning. While training should acknowledge that high volumes of deliberate practice in relevant activities are associated with improving skills (e.g., Catteeuw *et al.*, 2009), referees should also increase and maximize their deliberate experience and gain as much actual officiating as they can. The influence of context and realistic scenarios must be emphasized. Referee-coaches and officiating trainers may play the role not only of evaluators, but also as physical and decision-making coaches, designing, running and assessing training activities.

Development of evaluation systems

Referees face demands that are not necessarily observable or captured by ticks and marks. These skills and their relative importance to the overall proficiency of an official should be communicated to create an assessment, training and promotion system that is as transparent as possible. For example, Mascarenhas, Collins and Mortimer (2005) propose five cornerstones to the performance of rugby referees: (i) knowledge and application of the laws, (ii) contextual judgement, (iii) personality and management skills, (iv) fitness, positioning and mechanics and (v) psychological characteristics of excellence. These cornerstones of success for rugby referees provide specific areas for assessment and skill development. When evaluations are concrete but meaningful, assessors can direct officials to the tools for improvement. Moreover, as we mentioned above, teams of officials can be evaluated, where appropriate, to assess the impact of consistently training and performing together.

SUMMARY

Referees are involved in almost every kind of sport that is performed in a competitive manner. Unfortunately, many tasks of referees at times surpass the limited human capacity to process information.

Accordingly, a number of systematic judgement errors in referee decisions have been identified in the corresponding literature. Possible causes reside in early steps of information processing (e.g. the viewing position), in the application of inadequate knowledge (e.g. expectancies), as well as in incorrect rules of information integration (e.g. simple heuristics). On the basis of corresponding research, several measures and training methods have been proposed in order to improve the quality of referees' judgement and decision making.

Observers

8

Observers

Just as people in general, observers of sport events are strongly interested in understanding their environment. The observation of a sport competition provides a perfect opportunity to judge continuously the performances of athletes and to exchange these assessments. Of course, this contributes to the general fascination of sports. For example, spectators of a football match immediately express their evaluation of game situations, journalists evaluate football players' individual performances by giving them scores from 'very strong' to 'very poor' after each match and nowadays it is almost impossible to watch a game on the television without the commentaries of so-called experts who provide their expectancies and assessments, make predictions, criticize the referee and explain why the final score could only be as it is.

When compared with the research on JDM by athletes, coaches and referees, there are relatively few studies that are directly concerned with JDM by observers of sport events. Nevertheless, there are quite a number of interesting phenomena available in this area. Their significance derives partly from the fact, that they can be recognized to a certain extend also in the people who are directly involved in a competition. In addition, JDM of observers may have a direct influence on athletes' performance, for example, when supported by crowd noise. Finally, judgements of observers directly influence their own behaviour when

Judgement, Decision Making and Success in Sport, First Edition.
M. Bar-Eli, H. Plessner and M. Raab.

they decide to attend a game at all or if they invest in the growing betting market. This chapter provides an overview of some typical judgement biases of observers of sport events and their behaviour in the betting market.

BIASES IN JUDGEMENTS OF SPORT PERFORMANCE

In a classic study on group perception, Hastorf and Cantril (1954) studied evaluations of an exceptionally rough American football game between two university teams. A week after the game, students from each of the universities were asked about their reactions concerning the game. Among others, they were asked to judge how clean and fair as opposed to dirty and rough the game was. The majority of the students from the university who won the game tended to evaluate the game as fair and rough while the students from the university who had lost, found the game to be rather dirty and rough. In their explanation of this effect, Hastorf and Cantril (1954) focused on the constructive nature of social judgements, wherein judgements of people's behaviour are shaped by the observers' prior knowledge and values (cf. Chapter 2, Social cognition).

Of course, the study by Hastorf and Cantril (1954) can also serve as a typical example of 'motivated reasoning' (Kunda, 1990). People judge differently because they intend to favour different teams. However, as we mentioned before, many biases in human judgement are due to 'cold' aspects of human information processing and due to an important source of biases in the perceptual input. Accordingly, a case study by Schmidt and Bloch (1980) found that many differences in the evaluation of critical basketball situations between referees, coaches and observers are due to their different viewing positions.

We already mentioned the recent perspective of embodied cognition, that is, the relevance of perceptual and motor systems for the understanding of central cognitive processes (Raab, Johnson and Heekeren, 2009; see Chapter 5, How do athletes choose?). In line with this perspective, Maass, Pagani and Berta (2007) found that the same

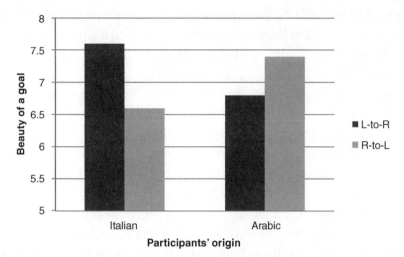

Figure 8.1   Beauty ratings for a goal that was either presented with a left-to-right or right-to-left trajectory by Italian and Arabic participants (Maass, Pagani and Berta, 2007).

athletic performance (a soccer goal) was perceived by Italian participants as stronger, faster and more beautiful, if presented with a left-to-right rather than right-to-left trajectory (see Figure 8.1). They argued that the direction in which language is written in a given culture produces a subtle bias in the interpretation of human action. The same action (e.g., athletic performance or aggression) will be perceived as more forceful when the spatial trajectory corresponds to the habitual writing direction. Consequently, the authors found an opposite directional bias with Arabic-speaking participants, suggesting that scanning habits due to writing direction are mainly responsible for the directional bias in person perception.

Viewing position and movement direction obviously limits the representativeness of an information sample. People are less aware of many other sources that can lead to a biased stimulus input. For example, Plessner *et al.* (2001) investigated the well-studied phenomenon of base-rate neglect (e.g., Bar-Hillel, 1980; see Chapter 6, Managerial JDM) in the judgement of a football player's quality. Their approach explained this finding as a sampling error in inductive judgements resulting from the confusion of predictor and criterion sampling in probability judgements. When given the task to judge a conditional probability, for example, the probability to drive drunk and have an accident, it makes a tremendous difference if you draw a sample depending on the predictor (driving drunk) or the criterion (having an accident). The latter sampling process leads to an overestimation of the conditional probability, because the rare criterion event 'accident' is overrepresented and the large number of people who drive drunk but do not have an accident are not considered. Plessner *et al.* (2001) applied this logic to the judgement of a football team's probability of winning a game given a certain player participated in a game. The environment they provided was such that the team hardly ever won a game. Thus, when participants sampled by the criterion the team's success, they overestimated the conditional probability and therefore the quality of the player just because they did not preserve the low environmental base rate of victories in their sample; that is, most cases, where the team lost and the player participated as well, were not considered. This bias did not show up when participants sampled by the predictor, the player's participation, which leads to a representative sample of victories and losses in this case and therefore to a fair estimate of the conditional probability.

A similar effect has been studied by Unkelbach and Plessner (2007) in another experimental application of the sampling approach (Fiedler, 2000) to judgements of sports performance, that is, the rating of a football player's ability. While most empirical work on the sampling approach is concerned with information sampling from the environment (e.g., Plessner *et al.*, 2001), this approach can also account for effects of selective sampling from memory (Unkelbach and Plessner, 2008). In order to test this assumption, Unkelbach and Plessner (2007) used a well-documented effect in social cognition research, the category-split effect. When people estimate the frequency of instances in a social category, the overall estimate is higher when the category is split into smaller sub-categories (Fiedler and Armbruster, 1994). The basic idea was that splitting a positive feature (e.g., excellent technical skills) of a player should result in a more favourable judgement when a negative feature (e.g., a lack of physical fitness) is not split and vice versa when the negative features are split and the positive features are not. In the experiment, sport coaches attended a presentation of a player, which, besides some background information about age, former clubs and so forth, contained an equal amount of positive and negative information. The former always related to his technical skill, the latter always related to his lacking fitness. After participants saw this presentation the crucial category-split manipulation followed. Half of the participants were assigned to a positive split condition and were asked about the player's pass-game, dribbling, shots and ball-security – all items that fell under the general category 'technical skill'. In comparison, they were asked about his 'physical fitness' in general. The remaining participants were assigned to a negative split condition and evaluated his 'technical skill' in general, whereas the category 'physical fitness' was split into the instances of speed, jump, stamina and aggressiveness. In the final overall evaluations, it was found that the player was evaluated more positively, when the positive category was split and more negatively when the negative category was split. As in the study by Plessner et al. (2001), participants were blind for this sampling manipulation and did not correct their judgements accordingly.

A rather negative feature of human memory is its susceptibility to intrusion errors and presupposition effects (e.g., Fiedler et al., 1996; Loftus, 1975). Such constructive memory effects have been studied in the domain of sports by Walther et al. (2002). In their experimental study, football experts and non-experts were presented with various scenes from a videotaped European Cup match. Among other manipulations, half of the participants were told after the video presentation that the team dressed in yellow won the match while the other half received the information that this team lost. Afterwards they were asked to rate the observed performance of the teams in yellow on various dimensions (e.g., ability and fight). It was found that experts were even more susceptible to the result-manipulation than non-experts. For example, when they believed that the yellow team won they were more likely to reconstruct the match in accordance with their implicit theory that a win on this level is rather due to an advantage in fighting than in ability. When they believed that the yellow team lost they rated its ability higher and its fighting during the game lower. Together, this study demonstrates that post-event information can exert an important influence on the evaluation of sport performance from memory.

The only other memory bias that has been studied in the domain of global judgement of sports performance so far refers to the use of the availability heuristic (see Chapter 2, Social cognition; Tversky and Kahneman, 1973). This heuristic allows people to base, for example, frequency judgement on the ease with which events can be retrieved instead of retrieving and counting all relevant instances. While this heuristic provides good results under many circumstances, it can also bias judgement if factors unrelated to the actual number of occurrences influence the retrieval process. For example, the ease with which the first (sensational) victory of Boris Becker in Wimbledon can be retrieved may lead to a relative overestimation of his weeks as world number one in comparison to the record of a player with less salient victories (e.g., Jim Courier). Indeed, Young and French (1998) found rankings of the greatest heavyweights of all time by noted boxing historians to be biased in line with the use of an availability heuristic, that is, fighters from more recent years were overrepresented in comparison to fighters who had their greatest time before the birth of the historians. One can easily imagine similar effects of availability on more short time rankings such as FIFA World Player of the Year.

A belief that many people involved in sports share is that athletes who started with an outstanding first season are susceptible to the so-called sophomore slump. The sophomore slump is a significant decline in performance during the second year (Taylor and Cuave, 1994). As with the hot-hand phenomenon, it has been argued that the sophomore slump does not really exist but that it is a cognitive illusion based on a lack of understanding of regression to the mean (Gilovich, 1984). According to this position, outstanding performances in the first year are just as likely to regress towards their actual level of ability as the statistical tendency of extreme scores to move towards the group means. However, in a careful analysis of the performance of 83 hitters and 22 pitchers who had an outstanding first year in the Major Baseball League, Taylor and

Cuave (1994) found a significant decline in the second year in the number of home runs. This trend is consistent with the assumption of a real sophomore slump. The results of other performance measures (batting average and runs batted in) were also consistent with the sophomore slump as with the regression to the mean explanation. Thus, people's failure to understand statistical tendencies together with some real declines in performance may jointly produce a stronger belief in the sophomore slump than would be warranted based on the actual career development of outstanding first year athletes alone.

In a similar vein, many other ideas people have about sports have been proved to be wrong. For example, Klaasen and Magnus (2007) found no statistical evidence for tennis experts' belief that it is an advantage to serve first in a set or with new balls. Neither are players more likely to lose their own serve after breaking their opponent's serve nor have top players a special ability to perform well at the 'big points'. Ayton and Braennberg (2008) analysed several beliefs about football. Again, they found no evidence for assumptions that a goal scored just before half time has a bigger impact on the result of a game than a goal scored at any other time for example, or that teams are more vulnerable after they scored a goal. This list could probably be continued with similar fallacies in many other sports. Apart from the fact that they illustrate people's limitations in dealing with statistical phenomena, they are also partly present because, as Klaasen and Magnus (2007) put it, commentators have plenty of time to fill.

Another well-known (cognitive) bias is the fundamental attribution error (or correspondence bias), that is, the tendency to attribute the behaviour of another person to dispositional (internal) factors, even when it is caused by situational (external) factors. Following the case of the sprinter Ben Johnson – who was stripped of his gold medal and world record in the 100-meter race at the Seoul Olympics after taking banned steroids – Ungar and Sev'er (1989) investigated the attributions made by college students regarding the causes of his behaviour. They found no evidence for the correspondence bias. On the contrary, participants attributed the doping behaviour of Ben Johnson less to internal (the athlete himself) than to external factors (e.g., sabotage).

This may be explained by the fact that participants were all Canadians and identified closely with Ben Johnson as a Canadian hero. In this case, internal attributions would have been self-threatening to participants. This explanation is supported by the fact that participants less concerned with the incident – that is, participants who probably identified less with the athlete – did not show this reversal of the fundamental attribution error. Thus, these results rather support the notion of a self-serving bias: a tendency to take credit for success and deny responsibility for failure (see Chapter 5, Judging one's own performance). Research suggests that this bias is not only frequently displayed by athletes but also by fans and the media (e.g., Lau and Russell, 1980; Peterson, 1980; Wann and Schrader, 2000).

PREDICTIONS AND BETTING

Prediction accuracy

Sport experts are required to evaluate the performance of an individual athlete or a team on a day to day basis. From an economic perspective this is important for prediction accuracy, as betting is an important aspect of the spectators' activities in sport participation. Some studies recently analysed the prediction accuracy of experts as well as what kind of information experts use to generate predictions (Andersson, Edman and Ekman, 2005; Pachur and Biele, 2007). The results mainly indicated that experts are not well enough prepared to predict outcomes of sport competitions and we do not know yet by which factors the prediction accuracy of these sport experts could be increased. One line of research argues that judgements become less biased when one gives deliberative thoughts to the judgement of others. This requires the use of valid information and analytically integrating this information (Vertinsky *et al.*, 1986). There is opposing evidence that less deliberative and more intuitive strategies are beneficial for predicting results of sport events. For instance, Halberstadt and Levine (1999) asked basketball experts to predict an upcoming outcome of a basketball game. Half of the participants were instructed to generate reasons about

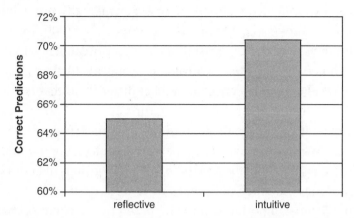

Figure 8.2 Percentage of correct predictions for the outcome of basketball games that were made in either a reflective or an intuitive mode by basketball experts (Halberstadt and Levine, 1999).

their choices, whereas the other half was asked to go with their gut-instinct and answer spontaneously. The results of this study showed that the basketball experts' rate of predicting the correct winners went up when they answered spontaneously (Figure 8.2). The authors summarized that analytical thinking reduces prediction accuracy in game outcomes. One potential explanation is that active reasoning reduces the use of potential relevant cues, such as feelings about the strength of a team, for participants' judgements. These feelings could accurately reflect multiple sources of acquired information about the strength of a team and could help with the accuracy of predictions (Betsch, Plessner and Schallies, 2004; Plessner and Czenna, 2008).

Research in psychology and economy has shown that the success of bettors depends on many different factors. Two important factors we focused on were the criteria which betting success was evaluated on and the competence of the bettors themselves.

One of these criteria for the evaluation of betting success are the motives of the bettors. For example, 'having fun' (motive) may reduce the validity of the money lost of won. The amount of correct predictions, the amount of money won and the relative success compared to guessing are now mainly used in betting models or in comparisons of different kinds of bettor groups. These criteria are used in real betting situations, experiments, simulations or experimentally produced stock markets (see Andersson, Memmert and Popowicz, 2009, for an overview). Prediction accuracy is used in a number of studies and it shows that the choice of the criteria above is relevant for further studies. For instance, results of an experiment or a bet differ if success is measured by predicting the correct result (e.g., in First-League-Football Cologne vs. Hannover at 1 : 3), by only predicting the winner (Hannover wins) or by predicting specific events (e.g., person/team to score the first goal). We will discuss later that the success of different groups of bettors partly depends on the influence of choices of criteria used.

One of the most important criteria for prediction accuracy of bettors is the success measured by the money that was won. Often absolute and relative gains are differentiated because bettors using professional bookmakers do not win large amounts of money in the long term. This is because the odds for individual competition bets or combinations of bets within a competition (e.g., world cups, leagues) and the fees to make a bet are set in favour of the bookmakers. Relative wins in comparison to a random prediction generator show that bettors usually do not have an advantage compared to the random generators (Cantinotti, Ladouceour and Jacques, 2004).

Another important criterion is the comparison of prediction accuracy of bettors with different kinds of models. General statistics, expert-based and mixed statistics-expert-based models as well as models that predict specific events or only use socio-economic factors can be differentiated (Lawrence *et al.*, 2006). Well-known statistics models derive ranks of individuals or teams. For example, in the football world ranking, nations are ranked based on the amount of games won and these are weighed due to the strength of opponents and importance of the game (see FIFA.com for the world ranking in football).

In individual sports such as tennis, rankings are needed to produce seedings (match-up plan) for tournaments and these seedings are used in order to compare predictions of bettors with the official rankings. Altogether statistical models sum up wins and losses as well as weigh up other relevant factors such as a home advantage, attack and defensive strengths (see Boulier and Stekler, 2003, for an overview). For obvious reasons, bookmakers keep their exact models secret, but it is known that they mix statistical models with expertise information.

A different class of models restricts the potential factors to predict sport event outcomes to a specific subset of criteria, which are all important to analyse, for instance, the number of gold medals won in the Olympics given socio-economic variables. This class of models can be described as a subset of statistical models often not only by restricting the set of factors but also the methods to derive predictions. Optimization is therefore limited due to the motivation to answer the influence of a set of parameters of interest. In economy, for instance, predictions on the rankings of nations are based on the number of medals won, they are optimized using the gross national product and the nations' population size or political system variables. Sometimes even quite complicated variables and sometimes more than 10 of them are combined, such as the relative size and number of months a nations has snow-covered areas in order to predict Winter Olympics gold medals (e.g., Johnson and Ali, 2004).

Psychological models often restrict their predictions to personal or situational relevant factors from which it is known that they influence choices in general and transfer them into event predictions (e.g., Nilsson and Andersson, 2010). However, comparisons between these classes of models have not been adopted much and require further investigations (Raab and Philippen, 2008).

An example for a personal relevant factor 'football knowledge' is often used. Researchers differentiate football knowledge by simply assessing self-judgement (Gröschner and Raab, 2006) by using a football knowledge test (Plessner and Czenna, 2008) or by showing that football tipsters for journals have a higher prediction accuracy in groups than as individuals (Forrest and Simmons, 2000).

In many studies, experts are no better than novices in predicting football game results (Andersson, Memmert and Popowicz, 2009; Cantinotti, Ladouceur and Jacques, 2004; Dijksterhuis, Bos, van der Leij and van Baaren, 2009; Gröschner and Raab, 2006, but see Pachur and Biele, 2007). Some previous findings were replicated in other domains and are of great interest as the predictions of experts seem to be counter-intuitive (Yates and Tschirhart, 2006). The result patterns and interpretations of the studies are not yet consistent in explanation for this effect. For instance, experts' predictions of hockey games show better predictions than those of novices, however, they do not outperform a random prediction model (Cantinotti, Ladouceour and Jacques, 2004). Football experts are better in predicting the correct game outcome, but, if they need to judge which teams will win, they are not better than novices (Andersson, Memmert and Popowicz, 2009).

Further studies showed that simple explanations do not solve the explanation problem as over- or underestimations (Koehler, Brenner and Griffin, 2002) and different information strategies were shown in the experiments (Bennis and Pachur, 2006; Gröschner and Raab, 2006; Scheibehenne and Bröder, 2007; Serwe and Frings, 2006). A limitation of most studies is that the groups are split in experts and novices purely based on their 'football knowledge'. Recently real bettor behaviour was studied and allowed better, more accurate analyses. For instance, Andersson (2008) showed that prediction accuracy for football game outcomes differed between tipsters for journals, bookmakers and betting experts. In an analysis of the men's world cup in football 2006 tipsters achieved a 55% prediction rate of correct outcomes and that did not differ significantly from simple statistical models such as using the FIFA ranking list for predictions. Still, bookmakers predicted better than tipsters did by integrating expert knowledge with huge sets of data (Lawrence *et al.*, 2006).

Betting behaviour of spectators

Betting behaviour of spectators has multiple facets. Here we will only focus on two important ones. First, what do we know about how spectators bet? This question alludes to the importance of the amount of bettors that wager, who bets and why. Second, how can we best describe the betting behaviour of different groups of bettors? This question alludes to the described differences between expert and novice bettors and differences in success between tipsters, bookmakers, models and spectators or just random predictions. Success, as previously discussed, will refer to the amount of money won, the number of correct predictions of winning teams or athletes as well as the correctly predicted scores of an event.

Based on this selection, we will not discuss facets of predictions such as the political discussion of legalization in betting (Hickman, 1976), the societal relevance and function of betting behaviour (Seelig and Seelig, 1998), betting addiction (Topf, Yip and Potenza, 2009) and illegal manipulations of games or legal issues (Folino and Abait, 2009) any further. We will rather provide examples on specific sports or specific competitions on national or international level, which are rather prototypical than detailed, since we are mainly concerned about the psychological aspects of betting behaviour for now.

How much money do spectators invest in betting?

Sport betting is one of the major branches and ranks second after lotteries regarding money spent. For instance in Germany, a country that only allows one bookmaker under public law, 6% of the adults (about 4 million people) place bets, based on a large survey by FORSA. Of these, 96% of the sport bets in Germany are set in football, Germany's most popular sport. Altogether over a billion Euros per year run into the wager industry of sport betting in Germany. These bets are based on estimates from both public and private bookmakers. These numbers are quite important for economic reasons as about 400 million Euros of these betting investments are directly transferred into sport sponsorship. On the international betting market, single events, such as the men's football world cup, have a total betting revenue of about 800 billion Euros.

Estimates from national statistic agencies are sometimes internationally compared and large samples such as surveys in Northern America report that about 13–20% of all bets are put in sports. Large variations can be found for the number of bets and the average wager of bets between studies and it obviously depends on whether samples are college students (Ellenbogen, Gupta and Derevensky, 2007) or pathological bettors (Blinn-Pike, Worthy and Jonkman, 2007). In some surveys, betting experience of adolescents or adults is estimated up to

80% (Welte *et al.*, 2008). Pathological prevalence scores in students range between 1% and 8% (Blinn-Pike, Worthy and Jonkman, 2007; Ellenbogen, Gupta and Derevensky, 2007) and in older adults between 0.5% and 2% (Clarke, 2008).

Who bets and why? There is a centre of research on betting behaviour in Northern America. Their data shows that betting of males out-numbers that of females by a multiple and also depends on the content of the bet (Ellenbogen, Gupta and Derevensky, 2007). Further studies split betting behaviour into socio-economic or cultural factors. For instance, Welte *et al.* (2008) combined social and personality factors providing correlations of both to lead to compulsive gambling.

Why do sport spectators bet? Previous research has indicated a number of motives as to why people bet. For instance, older adult bettors relax during betting exercises (Clarke, 2008) or follow their passion (Philippe and Vallerand, 2007). Adolescent and younger adults (mainly studied in college and university populations) mention motives of sensation seeking, winning money or social factors such as betting in their peer groups (Neighbors *et al.*, 2002).

Some findings show that systematic betting occurs less in athletes than in non-athletes (Welte *et al.*, 2008). College athletes present competitive reasons between athletes as well as motivation reasons to increase their effort in competitions (Curry and Jiobu, 1995).

All in all the field of describing and explaining betting behaviour in sports seems to be of growing interest. Nevertheless, the amount of studies conducted does not show a systematic and unifying approach. One reason for this is the lack of theorization and comparisons of approaches within and between the disciplines. There have recently been some attempts, at least for specific sports such as football, to compile different approaches (Andersson, Ayton and Schmidt, 2008).

SUMMARY

Research on judgement and decision making in observers received a growing interest in the last decades. Within the last years, a number of biases in perception, categorization and memory of observers have been demonstrated experimentally. Among others, observers of sporting contests frequently believe in correlations and phenomena that do not really exist (e.g., the hot hand). These biases occur during the evaluation of athletes' or teams' performance and may have important consequences for observers' behavior, for example if they are engaged in the betting market. In betting, the prediction accuracy depends on many factors. Some of them produce even counterintuitive results, such as that novices can predict the outcome of sport events as good or even better than experts. Differences between betting behavior on different levels of expertise as well as economic analyses of betting or psychological aspects of compulsive betting behavior gained more interest recently.

References

Abernethy B. (1990). Expertise, visual search and information pick-up in squash. *Perception*, *19*, 63–77.

Abernethy, B., Gill, D. P., Parks, S. L. and Packer, S. T. (2001). Expertise and the perception of kinematic and situational probability information. *Perception*, *30*, 233–252.

Abernethy, B. and Parker, S. (1989). Perceiving joint kinematics and segment interactions as a basis for skilled anticipation in squash. In C. K. Giam, K. K. Chook and K. C. The (eds), *Proceedings of the 7th World Congress in Sport Psychology*, Singapore, August 1989 (pp. 56–58). Singapore: International Society of Sport Psychology.

Abernethy, B. and Wood, J. M. (2001). Do generalised visual training programs for sport really work? An experimental investigation. *Journal of Sports Sciences*, *19*, 203–222.

Agor, W. H. (ed.). (1989). *Intuition in Organizations*. Newbury Park, CA: Sage.

Alain, C. and Sarrazin, C. (1990). Study of decision-making in squash competition: A computer simulation approach. *Canadian Journal of Experimental Psychology*, *15*, 193–200.

Allard, F., Deakin, J., Parker, S. and Rodgers, W. (1993). Declarative knowledge in skilled motor performance: Byproduct or constituent? In J. L. Starkes and F. Allard (eds), *Cognitive Issues in Motor Expertise* (pp. 95–108). Amsterdam, Netherlands: Elsevier.

Allard, F., Graham, S. and Paarsalu, M. L. (1980). Perception in sport: Basketball. *Journal of Sport Psychology*, *2*, 14–21.

Andersen, J. A. (2000). Intuition in managers. *Journal of Managerial Psychology*, *15*, 46–63.

Andersen, R. A., Snyder, L. H., Bradley, D. C. and Xing, J. (1997). Multimodal representation of space in the posterior parietal cortex and its use in planning movements. *Annual Review Neuroscience*, *20*, 303–330.

Anderson, N. H. (1981). *Foundations of Information Integration Theory*. New York, NY: Academic Press.

Andersson, P. (2008). Expert predictions of football: A survey of the literature and an empirical inquiry into Tipsters' and Odd-setters' ability to predict the world cup. In P. Andersson, P. Ayton and C. Schmidt (eds), *Myths and Facts About Football: The Economics and Psychology of the World's Greatest Sport* (pp. 257–281). Cambridge, UK: Scholar Press.

Andersson, P., Ayton, P. and Schmidt, C. (eds). (2008). *Myths and Facts About Football: The Economics and Psychology of the World's Greatest Sport.* Cambridge, UK: Scholar Press.

Andersson, P., Edman, J. and Ekman, M. (2005). Predicting the World Cup 2002 in soccer: Performance and confidence of experts and non-experts. *International Journal of Forecasting, 21*, 565–576.

Andersson, P., Memmert, D. and Popowicz, E. (2009). Forecasting outcomes of the World Cup 2006 in football: Performance and confidence of bettors and laypeople. *Psychology of Sport and Exercise, 10*, 116–123.

André, R. (2008). *Organizational Behavior.* Upper Saddle River, NJ: Pearson.

Anshel, M. H. (1991). A survey of elite athletes on the perceived causes of using banned drugs in sport. *Journal of Sport Behavior, 14*, 283–310.

Anshel, M. H., Williams, L. R. T. and Hodge, K. (1997). Crosscultural and gender differences on coping style in sport. *International Journal of Sport Psychology, 28*, 128–143.

Ansorge, C. J. and Scheer, J. K. (1988). International bias detected in judging gymnastic competition at the 1984 Olympic Games. *Research Quarterly for Exercise and Sport, 59*, 103–107.

Ansorge, C. J., Scheer, J. K., Laub, J. and Howard, J. (1978). Bias in judging women's gymnastics induced by expectations of within-team order. *Research Quarterly, 49*, 399–405.

Araújo, D. and Davids, K. (2009). Ecological approaches to cognition and action in sport and exercise: Ask not only what you do, but where you do it (Special issue). *International Journal of Sport Psychology, 40*(1).

Araújo, D., Davids, K. and Hristovski, R. (2006). The ecological dynamics of decision making in sport. *Psychology of Sport and Exercise, 7*, 653–676.

Araújo, D., Ripoll, H. and Raab, M. (eds). (2009). *Perspectives on Cognition and Action in Sport.* New York, NY: Nova.

Archer, E. A. (1980). How to make a business decision: An analysis of theory and practice. *Management Review, 69*, 54–61.

Armstrong, J. S., Denniston, W. B. and Gordon, M. M. (1975). The use of the decomposition principle in making judgments. *Organizational Behavior and Human Performance, 14*, 257–263.

Asch, S. E. (1946). Forming impression of personality. *Journal of Abnormal and Social Psychology, 41*, 258–290.

Ayton, P. and Braennberg, A. (2008). Footballers' fallacies. In P. Andersson, P. Ayton and C. Schmidt (eds), *Myths and Facts About Football: The Economics and Psychology of the World's Greatest Sport* (pp. 23–38). Cambridge, UK: Scholar Press.

Azar, O. H. and Bar-Eli, M. (2008). Biased decisions of professional football players: Do goalkeepers dive too much during penalty kicks? In P. Anderson, P. Ayton and C. Schmidt (eds), *Myths and Facts About Football: The Economics and Psychology of the World's Greatest Sport* (pp. 93–111). Cambridge, UK: Scholar Press.

Baker, J., Côté, J. and Abernethy, B. (2003). Sport specific training, deliberate practice and the development of expertise in team ball sports. *Journal of Applied Sport Psychology, 15*, 12–25.

Bakker, F. C., Whiting, H. T. and van der Brug, H. (1990). *Sport Psychology: Concepts and Applications.* Chichester, UK: John Wiley & Sons, Ltd.

Baldo, M. V. C., Ranvaud, R. D. and Morya, E. (2002). Flag errors in soccer games: The flash-lag effect. *Perception, 31*, 1205–1210.

Balmer, N. J., Nevill, A. M. and Lane, A. M. (2005). Do judges enhance home advantage in European championship boxing. *Journal of Sports Sciences, 23*, 409–416.

Bard, C., Fleury, M., Carrière, L. and Hallé, M. (1980). Analysis of gymnastics judges' visual search. *Research Quarterly for Exercise and Sport, 51*, 267–273.

Bar-Eli, M. (1984). Zur Diagnostik individueller psychischer Krisen im sportlichen Wettkampf: Eine wahrscheinlichkeitorientierte, theoretische und empirische Studie unter besonderer Berücksichtigung des Basketballspiels (The diagnosis of individual psychological crises in sports competition: A probabilistically oriented, theoretical and empirical study giving special attention to the game of basketball). Unpublished doctoral dissertation, Deutsche Sporthochschule, Köln, Germany.

Bar-Eli, M. (1991). On the use of paradoxical interventions in counseling and coaching in sport. *The Sport Psychologist, 5*, 61–72.

Bar-Eli, M. (1997). Psychological performance crisis in competition, 1984–1996: A review. *European Yearbook of Sport Psychology, 1*, 73–112.

Bar-Eli, M. (2001). Risk-taking strategies in sport and physical education: A theoretical model. *Sportwissenschaft, 31*, 72–81.

Bar-Eli, M. (2002). King Solomon in perspective: A response to Markus Raab. *Sportwissenschaft, 32*, 322–326.

Bar-Eli, M., Avugos, S. and Raab, M. (2006). Twenty years of 'hot hand' research: Review and critique. *Psychology of Sport and Exercise, 7*, 525–553.

Bar-Eli, M. and Azar, O. H. (2009). Penalty-kicks in soccer: An empirical analysis of shooting strategies and goalkeepers' preferences. *Soccer and Society, 10*, 183–191.

Bar-Eli, M., Azar, O. H., Ritov, I. *et al.* (2007). Action bias among elite soccer goalkeepers: The case of penalty kicks. *Journal of Economic Psychology, 28*, 606–621.

Bar-Eli, M., Galily, Y. and Israeli, A. (2008). Gaining and sustaining competitive advantage: On the strategic similarities between Maccabi Tel Aviv BC and FC Bayern München. *European Journal for Sport and Society, 5*, 75–96.

Bar-Eli, M., Lowengart, O., Master-Barak, M. *et al.* (2006). Developing peak performers in sport: Optimization versus creativity. In D. Hackfort and G. Tenenbaum (eds), *Essential Processes for Attaining Peak Performance (Perspectives on Sport and Exercise Psychology Series)*, Vol. 1, pp. 158–177). Oxford, UK: Meyer and Meyer.

Bar-Eli, M., Lowengart, O., Tsukahara, M. and Fosbury, R. D. (2008). Tsukahara's vault and Fosbury's flop: A comparative analysis of two great inventions. *International Journal of Innovation Management, 12*, 21–39.

Bar-Eli, M., Lurie, Y. and Breivik, G. (1999). Rationality in sport: A psychophilosophical approach. In R. Lidor and M. Bar-Eli (eds), *Sport Psychology: Linking Theory and Practice* (pp. 35–58). Morgantown, WV: Fitness Information Technology.

Bar-Eli, M. and Raab, M. (2006a). Judgment and decision making in sport and exercise: Rediscovery and new visions. *Psychology of Sport and Exercise, 7*, 519–524.

Bar-Eli, M. and Raab, M. (2006b). Judgment and decision making in sport and exercise (Special issue). *Psychology of Sport and Exercise, 7*(6).

Bar-Eli, M. and Raab, M. (2009). Judgment and decision making in sport and exercise: A concise history and present and future perspectives. In D. Araújo, H. Ripoll and M. Raab (eds), *Perspectives on Cognition and Action in Sport* (pp. 149–156). New York, NY: Nova.

Bar-Eli, M. and Schack, T. (2005). Group dynamics and team development in sport organizations. In C. Breuer and A. Thiel (eds), *Handbuch sportmanagement* (Handbook of Sport Management) (pp. 61–79). Schorndorf, Germany: Hofmann.

Bar-Eli, M. and Tenenbaum, G. (1989a). A theory of individual psychological crisis in competitive sport. *Applied Psychology, 38,* 107–120.

Bar-Eli, M. and Tenenbaum, G. (1989b). Observations of behavioral violations as crisis indicators in competition. *The Sport Psychologist, 3,* 237–244.

Bar-Eli, M. and Tenenbaum, G. (in press). Bayesian approach of measuring competitive psychological crisis. In G. Tenenbaum, R. Eklund and A. Kamata (eds), *Handbook of Measurement in Sport and Exercise Psychology.* Champaign, IL: Human Kinetics.

Bar-Hillel, M. (1980). The base-rate fallacy in probability judgments. *Acta Psychologica, 44,* 211–233.

Barnard, C. (1938). *The Functions of the Executive.* Cambridge, MA: Harvard University Press.

Baron, J. (2004). Normative models of judgment and decision making. In D. J. Koehler and N. Harvey (eds), *Blackwell Handbook of Judgment and Decision Making* (pp. 19–36). Malden, MA: Blackwell.

Baron, J. (2008). *Thinking and Deciding* (4th edn). New York, NY: Cambridge University Press.

Bennis, W. M. and Pachur, T. (2006). Fast and frugal heuristics in sports. *Psychology of Sport and Exercise, 7,* 611–629.

Bertrand, C. and Thullier, F. (2009). Effects of player position task complexity in visual exploration behavior in soccer. *International Journal of Sport Psychology, 40,* 306–323.

Betsch, T., Plessner, H. and Schallies, E. (2004). The value-account model of attitude formation. In G. R. Maio and G. Haddock (eds), *Contemporary Perspectives on the Psychology of Attitudes* (pp. 252–273). Hove, UK: Psychology Press.

Biddle, S. J. H., Hanrahan, S. J. and Sellars, C. N. (2001). Attributions: Past, present and future. In R. N. Singer, H. A. Hausenblas and C. Janelle (eds), *Handbook of Sport Psychology* (pp. 444–471). New York, NY: John Wiley & Sons, Inc.

Bird, E. J. and Wagner, G. G. (1997). Sport as a common property resource: A solution to the dilemmas of doping. *Journal of Conflict Resolution, 41,* 749–766.

Bless, H., Fiedler, K. and Strack, F. (2004). *Social Cognition: How Individuals Construct Social Reality.* Hove, UK: Psychology Press.

Blinn-Pike, L., Worthy, S. L. and Jonkman, J. N. (2007). Disordered gambling among college students: A meta-analytic synthesis. *Journal of Gambling Studies, 23,* 175–183.

Bouchard, R. A., Weber, A. R., Geiger, J. D. (2002). Review: Informed decision making on sympathomimetic use in sport and health. *Clinical Journal of Sports Medicine, 12,* 209–224.

Bouchard, T. J., Jr., Barsaloux, J. and Drauden, G. (1974). Brainstorming procedure, group size and sex as determinants of the problem-solving effectiveness of groups and individuals. *Journal of Applied Psychology, 59,* 135–138.

Boulier, B. L. and Stekler, H. O. (2003). Predicting the outcomes of National Football League games. *International Journal of Forecasting, 19,* 257–270.

Boyko, R., Boyko, A. R. and Boyko, M. G. (2007). Referee bias contributes to home advantage in English Premiership football. *Journal of Sports Sciences, 25*(11), 1185–1194.

Brand, R., Plessner, H. and Unkelbach, C. (2008). Basic psychological processes underlying referees' decision-making. In P. Anderson, P. Ayton and C. Schmidt (eds), *Myths and Facts About Football: The Economics and Psychology of the World's Greatest Sport* (pp. 173–190). Cambridge, UK: Cambridge Scholars Press.

Brand, R., Schmidt, G. and Schneeloch, Y. (2006). Sequential effects in elite basketball referees' foul decisions: An experimental study on the concept of game management. *Journal of Sport and Exercise Psychology, 28,* 93–99.

Brand, R., Schweizer, G. and Plessner, H. (2009). Conceptual considerations about the development of a decision-making training method for expert soccer referees. In D. Araújo, H. Ripoll and M. Raab (eds), *Perspectives on Cognition and Action in Sport* (pp. 181–190). Hauppauge, NY: Nova Sciences.

Brawley, L. R. (1984). Unintentional egocentric biases in attributions. *Journal of Sport Psychology*, *6*, 264–278.

Brisson, T. (2003). Experts' comments: Player's perspective. In J. L. Starkes and K. A. Ericsson (eds), *Expert Performance in Sports: Advances in Research on Sport Expertise* (pp. 216–218). Champaign, IL: Human Kinetics.

Bruine de Bruin, W. (2005). Save the last dance for me: Unwanted serial position effects in jury evaluations. *Acta Psychologica*, *118*, 245–260.

Bruine de Bruin, W. (2006). Save the last dance II: Unwanted serial position effects in figure skating judgements. *Acta Psychologica*, *123*, 299–311.

Brunswik, E. (1955). Representative design and probabilistic theory in a functional psychology. *Psychological Review*, *62*, 193–217.

Bunker, D. and Thorpe, R. (1982). A model for the teaching of games in the secondary school. *Bulletin of Physical Education*, *10*, 9–16.

Burns, B. D. (2004). Heuristics as beliefs and as behaviors: The adaptiveness of the 'hot hand'. *Cognitive Psychology*, *48*, 295–331.

Busemeyer, J. R. and Townsend, J. T. (1993). Decision field theory: A dynamic-cognitive approach of decision making in an uncertain environment. *Psychological Review*, *100*, 432–459.

Cacioppo, J. T., Priester, J. R. and Berntson, G. G. (1993). Rudimentary determinants of attitudes II: Arm flexion and extension have differential effects on attitudes. *Journal of Personality and Social Psychology*, *65*, 5–17.

Cañal-Bruland, R. (2009). Visual cueing in sport-specific decision-making. *International Journal of Sport and Exercise Psychology*, *7*, 450–464.

Cantinotti, M., Ladouceour, R. and Jacques, C. (2004). Sports betting: Can gamblers beat randomness? *Psychology of Addiction Behaviors*, *18*, 143–147.

Carron, A. V., Hausenblas, H. A. and Eys, M. A. (2005). *Group Dynamics in Sport* (3rd edn). Morgantown, WV: Fitness Information Technology.

Catteeuw, P., Helsen, W., Gilis, B. and Wagemans, J. (2009). Decision-making skills, role specificity and deliberate practice in association football refereeing. *Journal of Sports Sciences*, *27*, 1125–1136.

Chaiken, S. and Trope, Y. (eds). (1999). *Dual-Process Theories in Social Psychology*. New York, NY: Guilford Press.

Chambers, K. L. and Vickers, J. N. (2006). The effect of bandwidth feedback and questioning on competitive swim performance. *The Sport Psychologist*, *20*, 184–197.

Chandler, G. N. (1996). Business similarity as a moderator of the relationship between pre-ownership experience and venture performance. *Entrepreneurship: Theory and Practice*, *20*.

Chelladurai, P. (1990). Leadership in sports: A review. *International Journal of Sport Psychology*, *21*, 328–354.

Chelladurai, P. (1993). Leadership. In R. N. Singer, M. Murphey and L. K. Tennant (eds), *Handbook of Research on Sport Psychology* (pp. 647–671). New York, NY: Macmillan.

Chelladurai, P. (1999). *Human Resource Management in Sport and Recreation*. Champaign, IL: Human Kinetics.

Chelladurai, P. (2006). *Management of Human Resources in Sport and Recreation* (2nd edn). Champaign, IL: Human Kinetics.

Chelladurai, P. (2007). Leadership in sports. In G. Tenenbaum and R. C. Eklund (eds), *Handbook of Sport Psychology* (pp. 113–135). Hoboken, NJ: John Wiley & Sons, Inc.

Chelladurai, P. and Arnott, M. (1985). Decision styles in coaching: Preferences of basketball players. *Research Quarterly for Exercise and Sport, 56*, 15–24.

Chelladurai, P. and Haggerty, T. (1978). A normative model of decision-making styles in coaching. *Athletic Administration, 13*, 6–9.

Chelladurai, P., Haggerty, T. and Baxter, P. (1989). Decision style choices of university basketball coaches and players. *Journal of Sport and Exercise Psychology, 11*, 201–215.

Chelladurai, P. and Quek, C. B. (1991). Decision style choices of high school basketball coaches: The effects of situational and coach characteristics. *Journal of Sport Behavior, 18*, 91–108.

Chelladurai, P. and Riemer, H. A. (1998). Measurement of leadership in sport. In J. L. Duda (ed.), *Advances in Sport and Exercise Psychology* (pp. 227–253). Morgantown, WV: Fitness Informational Technology.

Chelladurai, P. and Saleh, S. (1978). Preferred leadership in sports. *Canadian Journal of Applied Sport Sciences, 3*, 85–92.

Chelladurai, P. and Saleh, S. (1980). Dimensions of leader behavior in sports: Development of a leadership scale. *Journal of Sport Psychology, 2*, 34–45.

Chi, M. T. H. (2006). Two approaches to the study of experts' characteristics. In K. A. Ericsson, N. Charness, P. Feltovich and R. Hoffman (eds), *The Cambridge Handbook of Expertise and Expert Performance* (pp. 21–30), New York, NY: Cambridge University Press.

Choi, N. J. and Kim, M. U. (1999). The organizational application of groupthink and its limits in organizations. *Journal of Applied Psychology, 84*, 297–305.

Clarke, D. (2008). Older adults' gambling motivation and problem gambling: A comparative study. *Journal of Gambling Studies, 24*, 175–192.

Coakley, J. J. (2006). *Sport in Society: Issues and Controversies* (9th edn). Boston: McGraw.

Cohen, M. D., March, J. G. and Olsen, J. P. (1972). The garbage can model of organizational choice. *Administrative Science Quarterly, 17*, 1–25.

Cooksey, R. W. (1996). The methodology of social judgment theory. *Thinking and Reasoning, 2*, 141–173.

Côté, J., Baker, J. and Abernethy, B. (2003). From play to practice: A developmental framework for the acquisition of expertise in team sports. In J. L. Starkes and K. A. Ericsson (eds), *Expert Performance in Sports: Advances in Research on Sport Expertise* (pp. 89–110). Champaign, IL: Human Kinetics.

Coulomb-Cabagno, G., Rascle, O. and Souchon, N. (2005). Players' gender and male referees' decisions about aggression in French soccer: A preliminary study. *Sex Roles, 52*, 547–553.

Courneya, K. S. and Carron, A. V. (1992). The home advantage in sport competitions: A literature review. *Journal of Sport and Exercise Psychology, 14*, 13–27.

Cray, D., Mallory, G. R., Butler, R. J. *et al.* (1988). Sporadic, constricted and fluid processes: Three types of strategic decision making in organizations. *Journal of Management Studies, 25*, 13–39.

Cray, D., Mallory, G. R., Butler, R. J. *et al.* (1991). Explaining decision processes. *Journal of Management Studies, 28*, 227–251.

Csikszentmihalyi, M. (1996). *Creativity, Flow and the Psychology of Discovery and Invention.* New York, NY: Harper Perennial.

Curry, T. J. and Jiobu, R. M. (1995). Do motives matter? Modeling gambling on sports among athletes. *Sociology of Sport Journal, 12*, 21–35.

Cyert, R. M. and March, J. G. (1963). *A Behavioral Theory of the Firm*. Englewood Cliffs, NJ: Prentice Hall.

Damisch, L., Mussweiler, T. and Plessner, H. (2006). Olympic medals as fruits of comparison? Assimilation and contrast in sequential judgments. *Journal of Experimental Psychology: Applied, 12*, 166–178.

Davis, J. H. (1992). Introduction to the special issue on group decision making. *Organizational Behavior and Human Decision Processes, 52*, 1–2.

de Fiore, R. and Kramer, T. J. (1982). The effect of team affiliation on perception in sports. *International Journal of Sport Psychology, 13*, 43–49.

Diederich, A. (1995). A dynamic model for multi-attributive decision problems. In J.-P. Caverni, M. Bar-Hillel, H. Barron and H. Jungermann (eds), *Contributions to Decision Making I* (pp. 175–191). Amsterdam, Netherlands: Elsevier Science Ltd.

Dijksterhuis, A., Bos, M. W., van der Leij, A. and van Baaren, R. B. (2009). Predicting soccer matches after unconscious and conscious thought as a function of expertise. *Psychological Science, 20*, 1381–1387.

Doherty, M. E. and Kurz, E. M. (1996). Social judgment theory. *Thinking and Reasoning, 2*, 109–140.

Drucker, P. (1966). *The Effective Executive*. New York, NY: Harper and Row.

Duda, R. O., Hart, P. E., Barrett, P. *et al.* (1976). *Development of the Prospector Consultation System for Mineral Exploration*. Menlo Park, CA: AI Center, SRI International.

Ebbeck, V. (1990). Sources of performance information in the exercise setting. *Journal of Sport and Exercise Psychology, 12*, 56–65.

Eddy, D. M. (1982). Probabilistic reasoning in clinical medicine: Problems and opportunities. In D. Kahneman, P. Slovic and A. Tversky (eds), *Judgment Under Uncertainty: Heuristics and Biases* (pp. 249–267). Cambridge, UK: Cambridge University Press.

Edwards, A. (1999). Reflective practice in sport management. *Sport Management Review, 2*, 67–81.

Edwards, W. (1954). The theory of decision making. *Psychological Bulletin, 51*, 380–417.

Edwards, W. (1962). Dynamic decision theory and probabilistic information processing. *Human Factors, 4*, 59–73.

Edwards, W. (1968). Conservatism in human information processing. In B. Kleinmuntz (ed.), *Formal Representation of Human Judgment* (pp. 17–52). New York, NY: John Wiley & Sons, Inc.

Edwards, W., Lindman, H. and Savage, L. J. (1963). Bayesian statistical inference for psychological research. *Psychological Review, 70*, 193–242.

Effenberg, A. O. (2005). Movement sonification: Effects on perception and action. *Multimedia, IEEE, 12*(2), 53–59.

Eiser, J. R. (1990). *Social Judgment*. Buckingham, UK: Open University Press.

Ellenbogen, S., Gupta, R. and Derevensky, J. L. (2007). A cross-cultural study of gambling behaviour among adolescents. *Journal of Gambling Studies, 23*, 25–39.

Elster, J. (1989). Social norms and economic theory. *Journal of Economic Perspectives, 3*, 99–117.

Elster, J. (1991). *Sour Grapes: Studies in the Subversion of Rationality*. New York, NY: Cambridge University Press.

Emmanouel, E. (1947). *History of Pharmacy*. Athens: Pryssos.

Ericsson, K. A. (1996a). The acquisition of expert performance: An introduction to some of the issues. In K. A. Ericsson (ed.), *The Road to Excellence: The Acquisition of Expert*

Performance in the Arts and Sciences, Sports and Games (pp. 1–50). Mahwah, NJ: Lawrence Erlbaum.

Ericsson, K. A. (ed.). (1996b). *The Road to Excellence: The Acquisition of Expert Performance in the Arts and Sciences, Sports and Games.* Mahwah, NJ: Lawrence Erlbaum.

Ericsson, K. A. (2003). Development of elite performance and deliberate practice: An update from the perspective of the expert performance approach. In J. L. Starkes and K. A. Ericsson (eds), *Expert Performance in Sports: Advances in Research on Sport Expertise* (pp. 49–84). Champaign, IL: Human Kinetics.

Ericsson, K. A., Krampe, R. T. and Tesch-Römer, C. (1993). The role of deliberate practice in the acquisition of expert performance. *Psychological Review, 100*, 363–406.

Ericsson, K. A. and Simon, H. A. (1993). *Protocol Analysis: Verbal Reports as Data.* Cambridge, MA: MIT Press.

Ericsson, K. A. and Williams, A. M. (2007). Capturing naturally occurring superior performance in the laboratory: Translational research on expert performance. *Journal of Experimental Psychology: Applied, 13*, 115–123.

Ernst, C., Olson, A. K., Pinel, J. P. J. *et al.* (2006). Antidepressant effects of exercise: Evidence for an adult-neurogenesis hypothesis? *Journal of Psychiatry and Neuroscience, 31*, 84–92.

Erpic, S. C., Wylleman, P. and Zupancic, M. (2004). The effect of athletic and non-athletic factors on the sports career termination process. *Psychology of Sport and Exercise, 5*, 45–59.

Everhart, B., Kernodle, M., Turner, E. *et al.* (1999). Gameplay decisions of university badminton students. *Journal of Creative Behavior, 33*, 138–149.

Farrow, D. and Raab, M. (2008). Receipt to become an expert in decision making. In D. Farrow, J. Baker and C. MacMahon (eds), *Developing Elite Sports Performers: Lessons from Theory and Practice* (pp. 137–154). New York, NY: Routledge.

Festinger, L. (1954). A theory of social comparison processes. *Human Relations, 7*, 117–140.

Fiedler, F. (1967). *A Theory of Leadership Effectiveness.* New York, NY: McGraw-Hill.

Fiedler, K. (1996). Explaining and simulating judgment biases as an aggregation phenomenon in probabilistic, multiple-cue environments. *Psychological Review, 103*, 193–214.

Fiedler, K. (2000). Beware of samples! A cognitive–ecological sampling approach to judgment biases. *Psychological Review, 107*, 659–676.

Fiedler, K. and Armbruster, T. (1994). Two halfs may be more than one whole: Category-split effects on frequency illusions. *Journal of Personality and Social Psychology, 66*, 633–645.

Fiedler, K. and Gebauer, A. (1986). Egozentrische Attributionen unter Fußballspielern (Egocentric attributions among soccer players). *Zeitschrift für Sozialpsychologie, 17*, 173–176.

Fiedler, K. and Juslin, P. (eds). (2005). *In The Beginning There is a Sample: Information Sampling as a Key to Understand Adaptive Cognition.* New York, NY: Cambridge University Press.

Fiedler, K. and Plessner, H. (2009). Induction: From simple categorization to higher-order inference problems. In F. Strack and J. Förster (eds), *Frontiers of Social Psychology: Social Cognition – the Basis of Social Interaction* (pp. 93–120). Philadelphia, PA: Psychology Press.

Fiedler, K. and Walther, E. (2004). *Stereotyping as Inductive Hypothesis Testing.* New York, NY: Psychology Press.

Fiedler, K., Walther, E., Armbruster, T. *et al.* (1996). Do you really know what you have seen? Intrusion errors and presuppositions effects on constructive memory. *Journal of Experimental Social Psychology, 32*, 484–511.

Findlay, L. C. and Ste-Marie, D. (2004). A reputation bias in figure skating. *Journal of Sport and Exercise Psychology, 26,* 154–166.

Fiske, S. T. and Neuberg, S. L. (1990). A continuum of impression formation, from category-based to individuating processes: Influence of information and motivation on attention and interpretation. In M. P. Zanna (ed.), *Advances in Experimental Social Psychology* (Vol. 23, pp. 1–74). New York, NY: Academic Press.

Fiske, S. and Taylor, S. E. (2008). *Social Cognition: From Brains to Culture.* New York, NY: McGraw-Hill.

Folino, J. O. and Abait, P. E. (2009). Pathological gambling and criminality. *Current Opinion in Psychiatry, 22,* 477–481.

Ford, G. G., Gallagher, S. H., Lacy, B. A. *et al.* (1997). Repositioning the home plate umpire to provide enhanced perceptual cues and more accurate ball-strike judgments. *Journal of Sport Behavior, 22,* 28–44.

Ford, G. G., Goodwin, F. and Richardson, J. W. (1995). Perceptual factors affecting the accuracy of ball and strike judgments from traditional American League and National League umpire perspectives. *International Journal of Sport Psychology, 27,* 50–58.

Forrest, D. and Simmons, R. (2000). Forecasting sport: The behaviour and performance of football tipsters. *International Journal of Forecasting, 16,* 317–331.

Frank, M. G. and Gilovich, T. (1988). The dark side of self- and social perception: Black uniforms and aggression in professional sports. *Journal of Personality and Social Psychology, 54,* 74–85.

Friedman, R. S. and Förster, J. (2000). The effects of approach and avoidance motor actions on the elements of creative insight. *Journal of Personality and Social Psychology, 79,* 477–492.

Gettys, C. F., Michel, C., Steiger, J. H. *et al.* (1973). Multiple-stage probabilistic information processing. *Organizational Behavior and Human Performance, 5,* 374–387.

Gigerenzer, G. (2000). *Adaptive Thinking: Rationality in the Real World.* New York, NY: Oxford University Press.

Gigerenzer, G. (2004). Fast and frugal heuristics: The tools of bounded rationality. In D. J. Koehler and N. Harvey (eds), *Blackwell Handbook of Judgment and Decision Making* (pp. 62–88). Malden, MA: Blackwell.

Gigerenzer, G., Todd, P. M. and ABC Research Group.(1999). *Simple Heuristics that Make us Smart.* Oxford, UK: Oxford University Press.

Gigone, D. and Hastie, R. (1997). Proper analysis of the accuracy of group judgments. *Psychological Bulletin, 121,* 149–167.

Gilbert, B. and Jamison, S. (1994). *Winning Ugly: Mental Warfare in Tennis – Lessons from a Master.* New York, NY: Fireside.

Gilis, B., Helsen, W., Catteeuw, P. and Wagemans, J. (2008). Offside decisions by expert assistant referees in association football: Perception and recall of spatial positions in complex dynamic events. *Journal of Experimental Psychology: Applied, 14,* 21–35.

Gilis, B., Weston, M., Helsen, W. *et al.* (2006). Interpretation and application of the laws of the game in football incidents leading to player injuries. *International Journal of Sport Psychology, 37,* 121–138.

Gilovich, T. (1984). Judgmental biases in the world of sport. In W. F. Straub and J. M. Williams (eds), *Cognitive Sport Psychology* (pp. 31–41). Lansing, MI: Sport Science.

Gilovich, T., Griffin, D. and Kahneman, D. (eds). (2002). *Heuristics and Biases: The Psychology of Intuitive Judgment.* New York, NY: Cambridge University Press.

Gilovich, T., Vallone, R. and Tversky, A. (1985). The hot hand in basketball: On the misperception of random sequences. *Cognitive Psychology*, *17*, 295–314.

Gobet, F. and Simon, H. A. (1996). Templates in chess memory: A mechanism for recalling several boards. *Cognitive Psychology*, *31*, 1–140.

Goldenberg, J., Lowengart, O., Oreg, S. *et al.* (2004). Innovation: The case of the Fosbury Flop. *Marketing Science Institute (MSI) Reports – Working Paper Series* (Issue 1, Report No. 04-106), 153–155.

Goldenberg, J., Lowengart, O., Oreg, S. and Bar-Eli, M. (2010). How do revolutions emerge? Lessons from the Fosbury Flop. *International Studies of Management and Organizations*, *40*(2), 30–51.

Goldstein, W. M. (2004). Social judgment theory: Applying and extending Brunswik's probabilistic functionalism. In D. Koehler and N. Harvey (eds), *Blackwell Handbook of Judgment and Decision Making* (pp. 37–61). Malden, MA: Blackwell Publishing.

Goldstein, W. M. and Hogarth, R. M. (1997). Judgment and decision research: Some historical context. In W. M. Goldstein and R. M. Hogarth (eds), *Research on Judgment and Decision Making: Currents, Connections and Controversies* (pp. 3–65). Cambridge, UK: Cambridge University Press.

Gordon, S. (1988). Decision styles and coaching effectiveness in university soccer. *Canadian Journal of Sport Sciences*, *13*, 56–65.

Gotwals, J. and Wayment, H. A. (2002). Evaluation strategies, self esteem and athletic performance. *Current Research in Social Psychology*, *8*, 84–100.

Gray, R. (2008). Multisensory information in the control of complex motor actions. *Current Directions in Psychological Science*, *17*, 244–248.

Greenberg, J. and Baron, R. A. (2007). *Behavior in Organizations* (9th edn). Upper Saddle River, NJ: Prentice Hall.

Greene, R. L. (1984). Incidental learning of event frequencies. *Memory and Cognition*, *12*, 90–95.

Greenlees, I. (2007). Person perception and sport performance. In S. Jovett and D. Lavallee (eds), *Social Psychology in Sport* (pp. 195–208). Champaign, IL: Human Kinetics.

Greenlees, I., Bradley, A., Holder, T. and Thelwell, R. (2005). The impact of two forms of opponents' non-verbal communication on impression formation and outcome expectations. *Psychology of Sport and Exercise*, *6*, 103–115.

Greenlees, I., Buscombe, R., Thelwell, R. *et al.* (2005). Perception of opponents in tennis: The impact of opponents' clothing and body language on perceptions of their playing ability. *Journal of Sport and Exercise Psychology*, *27*, 39–52.

Greenlees, I., Dicks, M., Holder, T. and Thelwell, R. (2007). Order effects in sport: Examining the impact of order of information presentation on attributions of ability. *Psychology of Sport and Exercise*, *8*, 477–489.

Gréhaigne, J. F., Godbout, P. and Bouthier, D. (1999). The foundations of tactics and strategy in team sports. *Journal of Teaching in Physical Education*, *18*, 159–174.

Griffin, L. A., Mitchell, S. A. and Oslin, J. L. (1997). *Teaching Sport Concepts and Skills: A Tactical Game Approach*. Champaign, IL: Human Kinetics.

Gröschner, C. and Raab, M. (2006). Vorhersagen im Fussball: Deskriptive und normative Aspekte von Vorhersagemodelle im Sport (Prediction in soccer: Descriptive and normative aspects of prediction models in sport). *Zeitschrift für Sportpsychologie*, *13*, 23–36.

Hackfort, D. and Schlattmann, A. (2002). Self-presentation training for top athletes. *International Journal of Sport Psychology*, *33*, 61–71.

Hagemann, N., Strauss, B. and Cañal-Bruland, R. (2006). Training perceptual skill by orienting visual attention. *Journal of Sport and Exercise Psychology, 28*, 143–158.

Hagemann, N., Strauss, B. and Leißing, J. (2008). When the referee sees red . . . . *Psychological Science, 19*, 769–771.

Halberstadt, J. B. and Levine, G. M. (1999). Effects of reasons analysis on the accuracy of predicting basketball games. *Journal of Applied Social Psychology, 29*(3), 517–530.

Hammond, K. R., Stewart, T. R., Brehmer, B. and Steinmann, D. (1975). Social judgment theory. In M. F. Kaplan and S. Schwartz (eds), *Human Judgment and Decision Processes* (pp. 271–312). New York, NY: Academic Press.

Hanin, Y., Korjus, T., Jouste, P. and Baxter, P. (2002). Rapid technique corrections using old way/new way: Two case studies with Olympic athletes. *The Sport Psychologist, 16*, 79–99.

Hastorf, A. H. and Cantril, H. (1954). They saw a game: A case study. *Journal of Abnormal and Social Psychology, 49*, 129–134.

Haubensak, G. (1992). The consistency model: A process model for absolute judgments. *Journal of Experimental Psychology: Human Perception and Performance, 18*, 303–309.

Heckhausen, H. (1989). *Motivation und Handeln* (2nd edn). Berlin, Germany: Springer.

Helsen, W. and Bultynck, J. B. (2004). Physical and perceptual-cognitive demands of top-class refereeing in association football. *Journal of Sport Sciences, 22*, 179–189.

Helsen, W., Gilis, B. and Weston, M. (2006). Errors in judging 'offside' in association football: Test of the optical error versus the perceptual flash-lag hypothesis. *Journal of Sport Sciences, 24*, 1–8.

Hickman, D. P. (1976). Should gambling be legalized for major sport events? *Journal of Police Science and Administration, 4*, 203–212.

Hickson, D. J., Butler, R. J., Cray, D. *et al.* (1985). Comparing one hundred fifty decision processes. In J. M. Pennings (ed.), *Organizational Strategy and Change* (pp. 114–142). San Francisco, CA: Jossey-Bass.

Hickson, D. J., Butler, R. J., Cray, D. *et al.* (1986). *Top Decisions: Strategic Decision Making in Organizations.* San Francisco, CA: Jossey-Bass.

Higgins, E. T. (1996). Knowledge activation: Accessibility, applicability and salience. In E. T. Higgins and A. W. Kruglanski (eds), *Social Psychology: Handbook of Basic Principles* (pp. 133–168). New York, NY: Guilford Press.

Hill, G. W. (1982). Group versus individual performance: Are *N*+1 heads better than one? *Psychological Bulletin, 91*, 517–539.

Hill, R. A. and Barton, R. A. (2005). Red enhances human performance in contests. *Nature, 435*, 293.

Hoberman, J. M. (1992). *Mortal engines: The Science of Performance and the Dehumanization of Sport.* New York, NY: Free Press.

Hodges, N. J. and Starkes, N. J. (1996). Wrestling with the nature of expertise: A sport specific test of Ericsson, Krampe and Tesch-Römer's (1993) theory of 'deliberate practice'. *International Journal of Sport Psychology, 27*, 400–424.

Hoffman, R. R. (1998). How can expertise be defined? Implications of research from cognitive psychology. In R. Williams, W. Faulkner and J. Fleck (eds), *Exploring Expertise* (pp. 81–100). Basingstoke, UK: Macmillan.

Hogarth, R. M. and Einhorn, H. J. (1992). Order effect in belief updating: The belief-adjustment model. *Cognitive Psychology, 24*, 1–55.

Horn, T. S. (2002). Coaching effectiveness in the sport domain. In T. S. Horn (ed.), *Advances in Sport Psychology* (2nd edn, pp. 309–354). Champaign, IL: Human Kinetics.

House, R. J. (1971). A path-goal theory of leader effectiveness. *Administrative Science Quarterly*, *16*, 321–338.

Huczynski, A. A. and Buchanan, D. A. (2007). *Organizational Behavior* (6th edn). Harlow, UK: Prentice Hall.

Isenberg, D. J. (1986). Group polarization: A critical review and meta-analysis. *Journal of Personality and Social Psychology*, *50*, 1141–1151.

Jackson, R. C. and Farrow, D. (2005). Implicit perceptual training: how, when and why? *Human Movement Science*, *24*, 308–325.

Jackson, R. C., Warren, S. and Abernethy, B. (2006). Anticipation skill and susceptibility to deceptive movement. *Acta Psychologica*, *123*, 355–371.

James, W. (1884). Absolutism and empiricism. *Mind*, 281–286.

Janelle, C. J., Duley, A. A. and Coombes, S. A. (2004). Psychophysiological and related indices of attention during motor skill acquisition. In A. M. Williams and N. J. Hodges (eds), *Skill Acquisition in Sport: Research, Theory and Practice* (pp. 282–308). London, UK: Routledge.

Janis, I. L. (1982). *Groupthink*. Boston, MA: Houghton Mifflin.

Johansson, G. (1973). Visual perception of biological motion and a model for its analysis. *Perception and Psychophysics*, *14*, 201–211.

Johnson, D. K. N. and Ali, A. (2004). A tale of two seasons: Participation at the Summer and Winter Olympic games. *Social Science Quarterly*, *85*, 974–993.

Johnson, J. (2008). Embodied cognition of movement decisions: A computational modeling approach. In M. Raab, J. Johnson and H. Heekeren (eds), *Progress in Brain Research: Mind and Motion: The Bidirectional Link between Thought and Action* (pp. 137–150). Amsterdam, Netherlands: Elsevier Press.

Johnson, J. and Raab, M. (2003). Take the first: Option generation and resulting choices. *Organizational Behavior and Human Decision Processes*, *91*, 215–229.

Johnson, J. G. (2006). Cognitive modeling of decision making in sports. *Psychology of Sport and Exercise*, *7*, 631–652.

Jones, M. V., Paull, G. C. and Erskine, J. (2002). The impact of a team's reputation on the decisions of association football referees. *Journal of Sports Sciences*, *20*, 991–1000.

Jussim, L. (1991). Social perception and social reality: A reflection-construction model. *Psychological Review*, *98*, 54–73.

Kahneman, D. and Miller, D. T. (1986). Norm theory: Comparing reality to its alternatives. *Psychology Review*, *93*, 136–153.

Kahneman, D., Slovic, P. and Tversky, A. (eds). (1982). *Judgment Under Uncertainty: Heuristics and Biases*. Cambridge, UK: Cambridge University Press.

Kahneman, D. and Tversky, A. (1979). Prospect theory: An analysis of decision under risk. *Econometrica*, *47*(2), 263–291.

Keating, J. W. (1964). Sportsmanship as a moral category. *Ethics*, *75*, 25–35.

Keeley, S. M. and Parks, J. B. (2003). Thinking critically about sport management. In J. B. Parks and J. Quarterman (eds), *Contemporary Sport Management* (pp. 79–94). Champaign, IL: Human Kinetics.

Kent, A. and Chelladurai, P. (2001). Perceived transformational leadership, organizational commitment and citizen behavior: A case study in intercollegiate athletes. *Journal of Sport Management*, *15*, 135–159.

Khatri, N. and Ng, H. A. (2000). The role of intuition in strategic decision making. *Human Relations*, *53*, 57–86.

Kious, B. M. (2008). Philosophy on steroids: Why the anti-doping position could use a little enhancement. *Theoretical Medicine and Bioethics, 29*(4), 213–234.

Klaasen, F. J. G. M. and Magnus, J. R. (2007). Myths in tennis. In J. Albert and R. H. Koning (eds), *Statistical Thinking in Sports* (pp. 217–240). Boca Raton, FL: Chapman and Hall.

Klein, G. (1989). Recognition-primed decisions. In W. B. Rouse (ed.), *Advances in Man–Machine System Research* (Vol.5, pp. 47–92). Greenwich, CT: JAI.

Klein, G. (2003). *The Power of Intuition: How to Use Your Gut Feelings to Make Better Decisions at Work*. New York, NY: Currency/Doubleday.

Klein, G., Wolf, S., Militello, L. and Zsambok, C. (1995). Characteristics of skilled option generation in chess. *Organizational Behavior and Human Decision Processes, 62*, 63–69.

Koehler, D. J. and Harvey, N. (eds). (2004). *Blackwell Handbook of Judgment and Decision Making*. Malden, MA: Blackwell.

Koehler, D. J., Brenner, L. A. and Griffin, D. (2002). The calibration of expert judgment: Heuristics and biases beyond the laboratory. In T. Gilovich, D. Griffin and D. Kahneman (eds), *Heurstics and Biases: The Psychology of Intuitive Judgment* (pp. 686–715). New York, NY: Cambridge University Press.

Kotter, J. P. (1990). *A Force for Change: How Leadership Differs from Management*. New York, NY: Free Press.

Kuhl, J. and Beckmann, J. (eds). (1994). *Volition and Personality: Action and State Orientation*. Seattle, WA: Hogrefe.

Kunda, Z. (1990). The case for motivated reasoning. *Psychological Bulletin, 108*, 480–498.

Kunda, Z. (1999). *Social Cognition: Making Sense of People*. Cambridge, UK: MIT Press.

Ladany, S. P. (2006). Introduction to a special issue on sport management. *International Journal of Sport Management and Marketing, 1*, 191–192.

Ladany, S. P. and Machol, R. E. (eds). (1977). *Optimal Strategies in Sports: Studies in Management Science and Systems*. Amsterdam, Netherlands: Elsevier/North-Holland.

Langley, A. (1989). In search of rationality: The purpose behind the use of formal analysis in organizations. *Administrative Science Quarterly, 34*, 598–631.

Lau, R. R. and Russell, D. (1980). Attributions in the sports pages. *Journal of Personality and Social Psychology, 39*, 29–38.

Laure, P. and Lecerf, T. (2002). Doping prevention among young athletes: Comparison of a health education-based intervention versus information-based intervention. *Science and Sports, 17*, 198–201.

Lawrence, M., Goodwin, P., O'Connor, M. and Önkal, D. (2006). Judgmental forecasting: A review of progress over the last 25 years. *International Journal of Forecasting, 22*, 493–518.

Leavitt, H. J., Dill, W. R. and Eyring, H. B. (1973). *The Organizational World*. New York, NY: Harcourt Brace Jovanovich.

Lehman, D. R. and Reifman, A. (1987). Spectator influence on basketball officiating. *The Journal of Social Psychology, 127*, 673–675.

Lewin, K. (1935). *A Dynamic Theory of Personality*. New York, NY: McGraw-Hill.

Liberman, N. and Trope, Y. (2009). The psychology of transcending the here and now. *Science, 322*, 1201–1205.

Loftus, E. F. (1975). Leading questions and the eyewitness report. *Cognitive Psychology, 7*, 560–572.

Lopes, L. L. (1991). The rhetoric of irrationality. *Theory and Psychology, 1*, 65–82.

Lopes, L. L. (1992). Three misleading assumptions in the customary rhetoric of the bias literature. *Theory and Psychology, 2*, 231–236.

Loy, J. W. (1981). Social psychological characteristics of innovators. *American Sociological Review*, *34*, 73–82.

Maass, A., Pagani, D. and Berta, E. (2007). How beautiful is the goal and how violent is the fistfight? Spatial bias in the interpretation of human behavior. *Social Cognition*, *25*, 833–852.

Machol, R. E., Ladany, S. P. and Morrison, D. G. (eds). (1976). *Management Science in Sports*. Amsterdam, Netherlands: Elsevier/North-Holland.

MacMahon, C., Helsen, W., Starkes, J. L. and Weston, M. (2007). Decision making skills and deliberate practice in elite association football referees. *Journal of Sports Sciences*, *25*, 65–78.

MacMahon, C. and Plessner, H. (2008). The sports official in research and practice. In D. Farrow, J. Baker and C. MacMahon (eds), *Developing Elite Sports Performers: Lessons from Theory and Practice* (pp. 172–188). London, UK: Routledge.

MacMahon, C. and Starkes, J. L. (2008). Contextual influences on baseball ball-strike decisions in umpires, players and controls. *Journal of Sports Sciences*, *26*, 751–760.

MacMahon, C. and Ste-Marie, D. M. (2002). Decision-making by experienced rugby referees: Use of perceptual information and episodic memory. *Perceptual and Motor Skills*, *95*, 570–572.

Magill, R. A. (2007). *Motor Learning and Control: Concepts and Applications*. New York, NY: McGraw-Hill.

March, J. G. and Simon, H. A. (1958). *Organizations*. New York, NY: John Wiley & Sons, Inc.

Markland, R. E. (1989). *Topics in Management Science* (3rd edn). New York, NY: John Wiley & Sons, Inc.

Markman, K. D. and Hirt, E. R. (2002). Social prediction and the 'allegiance bias'. *Social Cognition*, *20*, 58–86.

Martell, S. G. and Vickers, J. N. (2004). Gaze characteristics of elite and near-elite athletes in ice-hockey defensive tactics. *Human Movement Science*, *22*, 689–712.

Martens, R. (1987). Science, knowledge and sport psychology. *The Sport Psychologist*, *1*, 29–55.

Martin-Krumm, C. P., Sarrazin, P. G., Peterson, C. and Famose, J.-P. (2003). Explanatory style and resilience after sports failure. *Personality and Individual Differences*, *35*, 1685–1695.

Mascarenhas, D. R. D., Collins, D. and Mortimer, P. (2002). The art of reason versus the exactness of science in elite refereeing: Comments on Plessner and Betsch (2001). *Journal of Sport and Exercise Psychology*, *24*, 328–333.

Mascarenhas, D. R. D., Collins, D. and Mortimer, P. (2005). Elite refereeing performance: Developing a model for sport science support. *The Sport Psychologist*, *19*, 364–379.

Mascarenhas, D. R. D., O'Hare, D. and Plessner, H. (2006). The psychological and performance demands of association football refereeing. *International Journal of Sport Psychology*, *37*, 99–120.

Masters, R. S. W. (2000). Theoretical aspects of implicit learning in sports. *International Journal of Sport Psychology*, *31*, 530–541.

Masters, R. S. W. (2008). Applying implicit (motor) learning. In D. Farrow, J. Baker and C. MacMahon (eds), *Developing Elite Sports Performers: Lessons From Theory to Practice* (pp. 89–99). London, UK: Routledge.

Masters, R. S. W., Van der Kamp, J. and Jackson, R. C. (2007). Imperceptible off-center goalkeepers influence penalty-kick direction in soccer. *Psychological Science*, *18*, 222–223.

Mather, G. (2008). Perceptual uncertainty and line-call challenges in professional tennis. *Proceedings of the Royal Society B: Biological Sciences*, *275*(1643), 1645–1651.

McPherson, S. L. (1999). Tactical differences in problem representations and solutions in collegiate varsity and beginner female tennis players. *Research Quarterly for Exercise and Sport*, *70*, 369–384.

McPherson, S. L. and Kernodle, M. W. (2003). Tactics, the neglected attribute of expertise: Problem representations and performance skills in tennis. In J. L. Starkes and K. A. Ericsson (eds), *Expert Performance in Sports: Advances in Research on Sport Expertise* (pp. 137–168). Champaign, IL: Human Kinetics.

Meehl, P. E. (1954). *Clinical Versus Statistical Prediction: A Theoretical Analysis and Review of the Evidence*. Minneapolis, MN: University of Minnesota Press.

Mehrez, A., Friedman, L., Sinuany-Stern, Z. and Bar-Eli, M. (2006). Optimal threshold in multi-stage competitions. *International Journal of Sport Management and Marketing*, *1*, 215–238.

Memmert, D. and Roth, K. (2007). The effects of non-specific and specific concepts on tactical creativity in team ball sports. *Journal of Sports Sciences*, *25*, 1423–1432.

Miki, H., Tsuchiya, H. and Nishino, A. (1993). Influence of expectancy on opponents' competence upon information processing of their discrete attributes. *Perceptual and Motor Skills*, *77*, 987–993.

Mintzberg, H., Raisinghani, D. and Théorêt, A. (1976). The structure of 'unstructured' decision processes. *Administrative Science Quarterly*, *21*, 246–275.

Mirvis, P. H. (1998). Practice improvisation. *Organization Science*, *9*, 586–592.

Mohr, P. B. and Larsen, K. (1998). Ingroup favoritism in umpiring decisions in Australian Football. *The Journal of Social Psychology*, *138*, 495–504.

Morris, T. (2000). Psychological characteristics and talent identification in soccer. *Journal of Sports Sciences*, *18*, 715–726.

Mullen, B. and Riordan, C. A. (1988). Self-serving attributions for performance in naturalistic settings: A meta-analytic review. *Journal of Applied Social Psychology*, *18*, 3–22.

Munzert, J., Hohmann, T. and Hossner, E.-J. (2010). Discriminating throwing distances from point-light displays with masked ball flight. *European Journal of Cognitive Psychology*, *22*, 247–264.

Mussweiler, T. (2003). Comparison processes in social judgment: Mechanisms and consequences. *Psychological Review*, *110*, 472–489.

Mussweiler, T. and Strack, F. (1999). Hypothesis-consistent testing and semantic priming in the anchoring paradigm: A selective accessibility model. *Journal of Experimental Social Psychology*, *35*, 136–164.

Myers, D. (2002). *Intuition: Its Powers and Perils*. New Haven, CT: Yale University Press.

Neighbors, C., Lostutter, T. W., Cronce, J. M. and Larimer, M. E. (2002). Exploring college student gambling motivation. *Journal of Gambling Studies*, *18*, 361–370.

Nevill, A. M., Balmer, N. J. and Williams, A. M. (1999). Crowd influence on decisions in association football. *Lancet*, *353*, 1416.

Nevill, A. M., Balmer, N. J. and Williams, A. M. (2002). The influence of crowd noise and experience upon refereeing decisions in football. *Psychology of Sport and Exercise*, *3*, 261–272.

Nilsson, H. and Andersson, P. (2010). Making the seemingly impossible appear possible: Effects of conjunction fallacies in evaluations of bets on football games. *Journal of Economic Psychology*, *31*(2), 172–180.

Nocelli, L., Kamber, M., François, Y. *et al.* (1998). Discordant public perception of doping in elite versus recreational sport in Switzerland. *Clinical Journal of Sport Medicine, 8,* 195–200.

Nutt, P. C. (1993). The formulation process and tactics used in organizational decision making. *Organization Science, 4,* 226–251.

Nutt, P. C. (2002). *Why Decisions Fail: Avoiding the Blunders and Traps that Lead to Debacles.* San Francisco, CA: Barett-Kohler.

Orbach, I., Singer, R. N. and Murphey, M. (1997). Changing attributions with an attribution training technique related to basketball dribbling. *Sport Psychologist, 11,* 294–304.

Oudejans, R. R. D., Bakker, F. C. and Beek, P. J. (2007). Helsen, Gilis and Weston (2006) err in testing the optical error hypothesis. *Journal of Sports Sciences, 25,* 987–990.

Oudejans, R. R. D., Bakker, F. C., Verheijen, R. *et al.* (2005). How position and motion of expert assistant referees in soccer relate to the quality of their offside judgements during actual match play. *International Journal of Sport Psychology, 36,* 3–21.

Oudejans, R. R. D., Verheijen, R., Bakker, F. C. *et al.* (2000). Errors in judging 'offside' in football. *Nature, 404,* 33.

Over, D. (2004). Rationality and the normative/descriptive distinction. In D. J. Koehler and N. Harvey (eds), *Blackwell Handbook of Judgment and Decision Making* (pp. 3–18). Malden, MA: Blackwell.

Pachur, T. and Biele, G. (2007). Forecasting from ignorance: The use and usefulness of recognition in lay predictions of sports events. *Acta Psychologica, 125,* 99–116.

Paese, P. W., Bieser, M. and Tubbs, M. E. (1993). Framing effects and choice shifts in group decision making. *Organizational Behavior and Human Decision Processes, 56,* 149–165.

Parducci, A. (1965). Category judgment: A range-frequency model. *Psychological Review, 72,* 407–418.

Parducci, A. and Wedell, D. H. (1986). The category effect with rating scales: Number of categories, number of stimuli and method of presentation. *Journal of Experimental Psychology: Human Perception and Performance, 12,* 496–516.

Park, W. (1990). A review of research on groupthink. *Journal of Behavioral Decision Making, 3,* 229–245.

Parks, C. D. and Sanna, L. J. (1999). *Group Performance and Interaction.* Boulder, CO: Westview.

Paull, G. C. and Glencross, D. J. (1997). Expert perception and decision making in baseball. *International Journal of Sport Psychology, 28,* 35–56.

Pearson, R. and Petipas, A. (1990). Transition of athletes: Pitfalls and prevention. *Journal of Counseling and Development, 69,* 7–10.

Peterson, C. (1980). Attribution in the sports pages: An archival investigation of the covariation hypothesis. *Social Psychology Quarterly, 43,* 136–141.

Petlichkoff, L. M. (1988). Motivation for sport persistence: An empirical examination of underlying theoretical constructs. Unpublished doctoral dissertation, University of Illinois, Urbana-Champaign.

Philippe, F. and Vallerand, R. J. (2007). Prevalence rates of gambling problems in Montreal, Canada: A look at old adults and the role of passion. *Journal of Gambling Studies, 23,* 275–283.

Piirto, J. (1998). *Understanding Those Who Create* (2nd edn). Scottsdale, AZ: Great Potential.

Plessner, H. (1999). Expectation biases in gymnastics judging. *Journal of Sport and Exercise Psychology, 21,* 131–144.

Plessner, H. (2005). Positive and negative effects of prior knowledge on referee decisions in sports. In T. Betsch and S. Haberstroh (eds), *The Routines of Decision Making* (pp. 311–324). Hillsdale, MI: Lawrence Erlbaum.

Plessner, H. and Betsch, T. (2001). Sequential effects in important referee decisions: The case of penalties in soccer. *Journal of Sport and Exercise Psychology*, *23*, 200–205.

Plessner, H. and Betsch, T. (2002). Refereeing in sports is supposed to be a craft not an art: A response to Mascarenhas, Collins and Mortimer (2002). *Journal of Sport and Exercise Psychology*, *24*, 334–337.

Plessner, H., Betsch, C. and Betsch, T. (eds). (2008). *Intuition in Judgment and Decision Making*. New York, NY: Lawrence Erlbaum.

Plessner, H. and Czenna, S. (2008). The benefits of intuition. In H. Plessner, C. Betsch and T. Betsch (eds), *Intuition in Judgment and Decision Making* (pp. 251–265). New York, NY: Lawrence Erlbaum.

Plessner, H. and Haar, T. (2006). Sports performance judgments from a social cognition perspective. *Psychology of Sport and Exercise*, *7*, 555–575.

Plessner, H., Hartmann, C., Hohmann, N. and Zimmermann, I. (2001). Achtung Stichprobe! Der Einfluss der Informationsgewinnung auf die Bewertung sportlicher Leistungen (Beware of samples! The influence of sampling processes on the judgment of sport performance). *Psychologie und Sport*, *8*, 91–100.

Plessner, H. and Schallies, E. (2005). Judging the cross on rings: A matter of achieving shape constancy. *Applied Cognitive Psychology*, *19*, 1145–1156.

Plessner, H., Schweizer, G., Brand, R. and O'Hare, D. (2009). A multiple-cue learning approach as the basis for understanding and improving soccer referees' decision making. In M. Raab, J. Johnson and H. Heekeren (eds), *Progress in Brain Research: Mind and Motion: The Bidirectional Link between Thought and Action* (pp. 151–158). Amsterdam, Netherlands: Elsevier Press.

Pohl, R. F. (ed.). (2004). *Cognitive illusions: A Handbook on Fallacies and Biases in Thinking, Judgement and Memory*. Hove, UK: Psychology Press.

Raab, M. (2001). *SMART: Techniken des Taktiktrainings: Taktiken des Techniktrainings* (Dissertation). Köln, Germany: Sport und Buch Strauß.

Raab, M. (2002). T-ECHO: Model of decision making to explain behavior in experiments and simulations under time pressure. *Psychology of Sport and Exercise*, *3*, 151–171.

Raab, M. (2003). Implicit and explicit learning of decision making in sports is effected by complexity of situation. *International Journal of Sport Psychology*, *34*, 273–288.

Raab, M. (2007). Think SMART, not hard: Teaching decision making in sports from an adaptive cognition perspective. *Physical Education and Sport Pedagogy*, *12*, 1–18.

Raab, M. and Green, N. (2005). Motion as input: A functional explanation of movement effects on cognitive processes. *Perceptual and Motor Skills*, *100*, 333–348.

Raab, M. and Johnson, J. (2004). Individual differences of action-orientation for risk-taking in sports. *Research Quarterly for Exercise and Sport*, *75*, 326–336.

Raab, M. and Johnson, J. (2007). Option-generation and resulting choices. *Journal of Experimental Psychology: Applied*, *13*, 158–170.

Raab, M., Johnson, J. G. and Heekeren, H. R. (eds). (2009). *Mind and Motion: The Bidirectional Link Between Thought and Action* (*Progress in Brain Research*, Vol. 174). Amsterdam, Netherlands: Elsevier.

Raab, M., Masters, R. and Maxwell, J. (2005). Improving the how and what decisions of table tennis elite players. *Human Movement Science*, *24*, 326–344.

Raab, M. and Philippen, P. (2008). Auf der Suche nach der Einfachheit in Vorhersagemodellen im Sport. *Sportwissenschaft, 38*(4), 131–148.

Raab, M. and Reimer, T. (2007). Intuitive und deliberative Entscheidungen als Grundlage sportlicher Expertise (Intuitive and deliberative decisions as a basis of sports expertise). In N. Hagemann, M. Tietjens and B. Strauss (eds), *Psychologie der sportlichen Hoechstleistung* (Psychology of Elite Sports Performance). Goettingen, Germany: Hogrefe.

Rainey, D. W. and Larsen, J. D. (1988). Balls, strikes and norms: Rule violations and normative rules among baseball umpires. *Journal of Sport and Exercise Psychology, 10,* 75–80.

Rainey, D. W., Larsen, J. D. and Stephenson, A. (1989). The effects of a pitcher's reputation on umpires' calls of balls and strikes. *Journal of Sport Behavior, 12,* 139–150.

Rainey, D. W., Larsen, J. D., Stephenson, A. and Olson, T. (1993). Normative rules among umpires: The 'Phantom Tag' at second base. *Journal of Sport Behavior, 16,* 147–155.

Rains, P. (1984). The production of fairness: Officiating in the National Hockey League. *Sociology of Sport Journal, 1,* 150–162.

Rapoport, A. and Wallsten, T. S. (1972). Individual decision behavior. *Annual Review of Psychology, 23,* 131–176.

Rees, T., Ingledew, D. K. and Hardy, L. (2005). Attribution in sport psychology: Seeking congruence between theory, research and practice. *Psychology of Sport and Exercise, 6,* 189–204.

Reimer, T., Park, E. S. and Hinsz, V. B. (2006). Shared and coordinated cognition in competitive and dynamic task environments: An information-processing perspective for team sports. *International Journal of Exercise and Sport Psychology, 4,* 376–400.

Riggio, R. E. (2003). *Introduction to Industrial/Organizational Psychology* (4th edn). Upper Saddle River, NJ: Prentice Hall.

Ringrose, C. A. D. (1993). Enhancing creativity in athletes. In S. Serpa, J. Alves and V. Patco (eds), *Proceedings of the 8th World Congress of Sport Psychology* (pp. 282–285). Lisbon, Portugal: Technical University of Lisbon.

Ripoll, H. (1988). Analysis of visual scanning patterns of volleyball players in a problem solving task. *International Journal of Sport Psychology, 19,* 9–25.

Ripoll, H. (ed.). (1991). Information processing and decision making in sport (Special Issue). *International Journal of Sport Psychology, 22*(13).

Ritov, I. and Baron, J. (1990). Reluctance to vaccinate: Omission bias and ambiguity. *Journal of Behavioral Decision Making, 3,* 263–277.

Ritov, I. and Baron, J. (1992). Status-quo and omission biases. *Journal of Risk and Uncertainty, 5,* 49–61.

Ritov, I. and Baron, J. (1995). Outcome knowledge, regret and omission bias. *Organizational Behavior and Human Decision Processes, 64,* 119–127.

Robbins, S. P. (2005). *Organizational Behavior* (11th edn). Upper Saddle River, NJ: Pearson.

Salmela, J. H. (1978). Gymnastics judging: A complex information processing task, or (who's putting one over on who?) Part 1 and 2. *International Gymnast, 20,* 54–56 and 62–63.

Samuelson, P. A. and Nordhaus, W. D. (2004). *Economics* (18th edn). New York, NY: McGraw-Hill/Irwin.

Sanders, R. (1999). *The Executive Decision-making Process: Identifying Problems and Assessing Outcomes.* Westport, CT: Quorum.

Savelsbergh, G. J. P., Van der Kamp, J., Williams, A. M. and Ward, P. (2005). Anticipation and visual search behaviour in expert soccer goalkeepers. *Ergonomics*, *48*, 1686–1697.

Scheer, J. K. (1973). Effect of placement in the order of competition on scores of Nebraska high school students. *Research Quarterly*, *44*, 79–85.

Scheer, J. K. and Ansorge, C. J. (1975). Effects of naturally induced judges' expectations on the ratings of physical performances. *Research Quarterly*, *46*, 463–470.

Scheer, J. K. and Ansorge, C. J. (1979). Influence due to expectations of judges: A function of internal–external locus of control. *Journal of Sport Psychology*, *1*, 53–58.

Scheer, J. K., Ansorge, C. J. and Howard, J. (1983). Judging bias induced by viewing contrived videotapes: A function of selected psychological variables. *Journal of Sport Psychology*, *5*, 427–437.

Scheibehenne, B. and Bröder, A. (2007). Predicting Wimbledon 2005 tennis results by mere player name recognition. *International Journal of Forecasting*, *23*, 415–426.

Schermerhorn, J. R., Hunt, J. G. and Osborn, R. N. (2003). *Organizational Behavior* (8th edn). Hoboken, NJ: John Wiley & Sons, Inc.

Schmidt, G. and Bloch, M. (1980). Warum gibt es ein Schiedsrichterproblem? Bericht über eine Fallstudie (Why does a referee problem exist? Report on a case study). *Leistungssport*, *10*, 290–299.

Schmidt, R. A. (1975). A schema theory of discrete motor skill learning. *Psychological Review*, *82*, 225–260.

Schmole, M. (2000). Synergetische Sportspielmethodik (Synergetical method of teaching sport games). *Sportonomics*, *6*, 41–47.

Schwartz, S. M., Baron, J. and Clarke, J. R. (1988). A causal Bayesian model for the diagnosis of appendicitis. In J. F. Lemmer and L. N. Kanal (eds), *Uncertainty in Artificial Intelligence* (Vol. 2, pp. 423–434). Amsterdam, Netherlands: North Holland.

Schwarz, W. (2011). Compensating tendencies in penalty kick decisions of referees in professional football: Evidence from the German Bundesliga 1963–2006. *Journal of Sports Sciences*, *29*(5), 441–447.

Schweizer, G., Plessner, H. and Brand, R. (2010). Studying experts' intuitive decision making online using video stimuli. In A. Glöckner and C. Witteman (eds), *Foundations for Tracing Intuition: Challenges and Methods* (pp. 106–122). Hove, UK: Psychology Press.

Schweizer, G., Plessner, H., Kahlert, D. and Brand, R. (2011). A video-based training method for improving soccer referees' intuitive decision-making skills. *Journal of Applied Sport Psychology*, *23*.

Scott, D. K. (1999). A multiframe perspective of leadership and organizational climate in intercollegiate athletics. *Journal of Sport Management*, *13*, 298–316.

Seelig, M. and Seelig, J. (1998). Gambling, government and society. *Canadian Public Policy*, *24*, 177–181.

Seligman, M. E., Nolen-Hoeksema, S., Thornton, N. and Thornton, K. M. (1990). Explanatory style as a mechanism of disappointing athletic performance. *Psychological Science*, *1*, 143–146.

Seltzer, R. and Glass, W. (1991). International politics and judging in Olympic skating events. *Journal of Sport Behavior*, *14*, 189–200.

Serwe, S. and Frings, C. (2006). Who will win Wimbledon? The recognition heuristic in predicting sports events. *Journal of Behavioral Decision Making*, *19*, 321–332.

Sheldon, J. P. (2003). Self-evaluation of competence by adult athletes: Its relation to skill level and personal importance. *Sport Psychologist*, *17*, 426–443.

Sherman, D. K. and Kim, H. S. (2005). Is there an 'I' in 'team'? The role of the self in group-serving judgments. *Journal of Personality and Social Psychology*, *88*, 108–120.

Simon, H. A. (1945). *Administrative Behavior*. New York, NY: Free Press.

Simon, H. A. (1955). A behavioral model of rational choice. *Quarterly Journal of Economics*, *69*, 99–118.

Simon, H. A. (1956). Rational choice and the structure of the environment. *Psychological Review*, *63*, 129–138.

Simon, H. A. (1960). *The New Science of Management Decisions*. Englewood Cliffs, NJ: Prentice Hall.

Simon, H. A. (1982). *Models of Bounded Rationality*. Cambridge, MA: MIT Press.

Simon, H. A. (1987). Bounded rationality. In J. Eatwell, M. Milgate and P. Newman (eds), *The New Palgrave: A Dictionary of Economics* (pp. 266–268). London, UK: Macmillan.

Simon, P., Striegel, H., Aust, F. *et al.* (2006). Doping in fitness sports: Estimated number of unreported cases and individual probability of doping. *Addiction*, *101*, 1640–1644.

Singer, R. N., Cauraugh, J. H., Murphy, M. *et al.* (1991). Attentional control, distractors and motor performance. *Human Performance*, *4*, 55–69.

Singer, R. N., Murphy, M. and Tennant, L. K. (eds). (1993). *Handbook of Research on Sport Psychology*. New York, NY: Macmillan.

Sinuany-Stern, Z., Israeli, Y. and Bar-Eli, M. (2006). Application of the analytic hierarchy process for the evaluation of basketball teams. *International Journal of Sport Management and Marketing*, *1*, 193–207.

Slack, T. and Parent, M. M. (2006). *Understanding Sport Organizations: The Application of Organization Theory* (2nd edn). Champaign, IL: Human Kinetics.

Slovic, P. and Lichtenstein, S. (1971). Comparison of Bayesian and regression approaches to the study of information processing in judgment. *Organizational Behavior and Human Performance*, *6*, 649–744.

Slovic, P., Fischhoff, B. and Lichtenstein, S. (1977). Behavioral decision theory. *Annual Review of Psychology*, *28*, 1–39.

Smart, D. L. and Wolfe, R. A. (2003). The contribution of leadership and human resources to organizational success: An empirical assessment of performance in major league baseball. *European Sport Management Quarterly*, *3*, 165–188.

Smeeton N., Ward P. and Williams A. M. (2004). Transfer of perceptual skill in a real-world task: Training, instruction and transfer in tennis. *Journal of Experimental Psychology: Applied*, *8*, 259–270.

Smith, G. (1999). Resilience concept and findings: Implications for family therapy. *Journal of Family Therapy*, *21*, 154–158.

Smith, R. E. (1999). The sport psychologist as scientist-practitioner: Reciprocal relations linking theory, research and intervention. In R. Lidor and M. Bar-Eli (eds), *Sport Psychology: Linking Theory and Practice* (pp. 15–34). Morgantown, WV: Fitness Information Technology.

Smith, R. E. and Christensen, D. S. (1995). Psychological skills as predictors of performance and survival in professional baseball. *Journal of Sport and Exercise Psychology*, *17*, 399–415.

Smith, R. E., Smoll, F. L. and Curtis, B. (1978). Coaching behaviors in little league baseball. In F. L. Smoll and R. E. Smith (eds), *Psychological Perspectives in Youth Sports* (pp. 173–201). Washington, DC: Hemisphere.

Smith, R. E., Smoll, F. L. and Hunt, E. B. (1977). A system for the behavioral assessment of athletic coaches. *Research Quarterly, 48*, 401–407.

Smith, R. W. (1986). Toward a cognitive-affective model of athletic burnout. *Journal of Sport Psychology, 8*, 36–50.

Smoll, F. L. and Smith, R. E. (1989). Leadership behaviors in sport: A theoretical model and research paradigm. *Journal of Applied Social Psychology, 19*, 1522–1551.

Soberlak, P. and Côté, J. (2003). The developmental activities of elite ice hockey players. *Journal of Applied Sport Psychology, 15*, 41–49.

Soelberg, P. (1966). Unprogrammed decision making. *Academy of Management Proceedings*, 3–16.

Souchon, N., Coulomb-Cabagno, G., Traclet, A. and Rascle, O. (2004). Referees' decision making in handball and transgressive behaviors: Influence of stereotypes about gender of players? *Sex Roles, 51*, 445–453.

Spence, J. and Spence, K. (1966). The motivational components of manifest anxiety: Drive and drive stimuli. In C. D. Spielberger (ed.), *Anxiety and Behavior* (pp. 291–326). New York, NY: Academic Press.

Stacey, R. D. (2007). *Strategic Management and Organizational Dynamics: The Challenges of Complexity* (5th edn). Harlow, UK: Prentice Hall.

Starkes, J. L. and Ericsson, K. A. (eds). (2003). *Expert Performance in Sports: Advances in Research on Sport Expertise*. Champaign, IL: Human Kinetics.

Stefani, R. (1998). Predicting outcomes. In J. Bennett (ed.), *Statistics in Sport* (pp. 249–275). London, UK: Arnold.

Ste-Marie, D. (1996). International bias in gymnastic judging: Conscious or unconscious influences? *Perceptual and Motor Skills, 83*, 963–975.

Ste-Marie, D. (1999). Expert–novice differences in gymnastic judging: An information processing perspective. *Applied Cognitive Psychology, 13*, 269–281.

Ste-Marie, D. (2000). Expertise in women's gymnastic judging: An observational approach. *Perceptual and Motor Skills, 90*, 543–546.

Ste-Marie, D. (2003a). Memory biases in gymnastic judging: Differential effects of surface feature changes. *Applied Cognitive Psychology, 17*, 733–751.

Ste-Marie, D. (2003b). Expertise in sport judges and referees: Circumventing information-processing limitations. In J. L. Starkes and A. Ericsson (eds), *Expert Performance in Sport: Advances in Research on Sport Expertise* (pp. 169–190). Champaign IL: Human Kinetics.

Ste-Marie, D. and Lee, T. D. (1991). Prior processing effect on gymnastic judging. *Journal of Experimental Psychology: Learning, Memory and Cognition, 17*, 126–136.

Ste-Marie, D. and Valiquette, S. M. (1996). Enduring memory-influenced biases in gymnastic judging. *Journal of Experimental Psychology: Learning, Memory and Cognition, 22*, 1498–1502.

Ste-Marie, D., Valiquette, S. M. and Taylor, G. (2001). Memory-influenced biases in gymnastic judging occur across different prior processing conditions. *Research Quarterly for Exercise and Sport, 72*, 420–426.

Sternberg, R. J. (1993). Procedures for identifying intellectual potential in the gifted: A perspective on alternative 'metaphors of mind.' In K. A. Heller, F. J. Monks and A. H. Passow (eds), *International Handbook of Research and Development of Giftedness and Talent* (pp. 185–208). Oxford, UK: Pergamon.

Stewart, G. L., Manz, C. C. and Sims, H. P. (1998). *Team Work and Group Dynamics*. New York, NY: John Wiley & Sons, Inc.

Stone, J., Perry, Z. W. and Darley, J. M. (1997). 'White men can't jump': Evidence for the perceptual confirmation of racial stereotypes following a basketball game. *Basic and Applied Social Psychology*, *19*, 291–306.

Straub, W. F. and Williams, J. M. (eds). (1984). *Cognitive Sport Psychology*. Lansing, MI: Sport Science.

Sudgen, R. (1991). Rational choice: A survey. *Economic Journal*, *101*, 751–783.

Sutter, M. and Kocher, M. G. (2004). Favoritism of agents: The case of referees' home bias. *Journal of Economic Psychology*, *25*, 461–469.

Tajfel, H. and Wilkes, A.-L. (1963). Classification and quantitative judgement. *British Journal of Psychology*, *54*, 101–114.

Taylor, J. and Cuave, K. L. (1994). The sophomore slump among professional baseball players: Real or imagined? *International Journal of Sport Psychology*, *25*, 230–239.

Teipel, D., Gerisch, G. and Busse, M. (1983). Evaluation of aggressive behavior in football. *International Journal of Sport Psychology*, *14*, 228–242.

Tenenbaum, G. (2003). Expert athletes: An integrated approach to decision making. In J. L. Starkes and K. A. Ericsson (eds), *Expert Performance in Sports: Advances in Research on Sport Expertise* (pp. 191–218). Champaign, IL: Human Kinetics.

Tenenbaum, G. and Bar-Eli, M. (1993). Decision making in sport: A cognitive perspective. In R. N. Singer, M. Murphey and L. K. Tennant (eds), *Handbook of Research on Sport Psychology* (pp. 171–192). New York, NY: Macmillan.

Tenenbaum, G. and Bar-Eli, M. (1995). Contemporary issues in exercise and sport psychology research. In S. J. H. Biddle (ed.), *European Perspectives on Sport and Exercise Psychology* (pp. 292–323). Champaign, IL: Human Kinetics.

Tenenbaum, G. and Eklund, R. C. (eds). (2007). *Handbook of Sport Psychology*. Hoboken, NJ: John Wiley & Sons, Inc.

Tenenbaum, G., Eklund, R. and Kamata, A. (eds). (in press). *Handbook of Measurement in Sport and Exercise Psychology*. Champaign, IL: Human Kinetics.

Tenenbaum, G. and Lidor, R. (2005). Research on decision-making and the use of cognitive strategies in sport settings. In D. Hackfort, J. L. Duda and R. Lidor (eds), *Handbook of Research in Applied Sport Psychology: International Perspectives* (pp. 75–91). Morgantown, WV: Fitness Information Technology.

Thibaut, J. W. and Kelley, H. H. (1959). *The Social Psychology of Groups*. New York, NY: John Wiley & Sons, Inc.

Tiryaki, M. (2005). Assessing whether black uniforms affect the decisions of Turkish soccer referees: Is the finding of Frank and Gilovich's study valid for Turkish culture? *Perceptual and Motor Skills*, *100*, 51–57.

Topf, J. L., Yip, S. W. and Potenza, M. N. (2009). Pathological gambling: Biological and clinical considerations. *Journal of Addiction Medicine*, *3*(3), 111–119.

Townsend, J. T. and Busemeyer, J. R. (1995). Dynamic representation of decision-making. In R. F. Port and T. van Gelder (eds), *Mind as Motion: Explorations in the Dynamics of Cognition* (pp. 101–120). Cambridge, MA: MIT Press.

Tversky, A. and Kahneman, D. (1973). Availability: A heuristic for judging frequency and probability. *Cognitive Psychology*, *5*, 207–232.

Tversky, A. and Kahneman, D. (1982). Judgments of and by representativeness. In D. Kahneman, P. Slovic and A. Tversky (eds), *Judgment Under Uncertainty: Heuristics and Biases* (pp. 84–98). Cambridge, UK: Cambridge University Press.

Tversky, A. and Kahneman, D. (1992). Advances in prospect-theory: Cumulative representation of uncertainty. *Journal of Risk and Uncertainty*, 5, 297–323.

Ungar, S. and Sev'er, A. (1989). 'Say it ain't so, Ben': Attributions for a fallen hero. *Social Psychology Quarterly*, 52, 207–212.

Unkelbach, C. and Memmert, D. (2008). Game-management, context-effects and calibration: The case of yellow cards in soccer. *Journal of Sport and Exercise Psychology*, 30, 95–109.

Unkelbach, C. and Memmert, D. (2010). Crowd noise as a cue in referee decisions contributes to the home advantage. *Journal of Sport and Exercise Psychology*, 32, 483–498.

Unkelbach, C. and Plessner, H. (2007). 'Category-Split' bei Urteilen über Sportler und Sportarten (Category split in judgments about sportsmen and sports). *Zeitschrift für Sozialpsychologie*, 38, 111–121.

Unkelbach, C. and Plessner, H. (2008). The sampling trap of intuitive judgments: Can reflection reach beyond sampling constraints? In H. Plessner, C. Betsch and T. Betsch (eds), *Intuition in Judgment and Decision Making* (pp. 283–294). Mahwah, NJ: Lawrence Erlbaum.

Van den Auweele, Y., Boen, F., De Geest, A. and Feys, J. (2004). Judging bias in synchronized swimming: Open feedback leads to nonperformance-based conformity. *Journal of Sport and Exercise Psychology*, 26, 561–571.

Van Quaquebeke, N. and Giessner, S. R. (2010). How embodied cognition affect judgments: Height-related attribution bias in football foul calls. *Journal of Sport and Exercise Psychology*, 32, 3–22.

Van Yperen, N. W. (1992). Self-enhancement among major league soccer players: The role of importance and ambiguity on social comparison behavior. *Journal of Applied Social Psychology*, 22, 1186–1198.

Vertinsky, P., Kanetkar, V., Vertinsky, I. and Wilson, G. (1986). Prediction of wins and losses in a series of field hockey games: A study of probability assessment quality and cognitive information-processing models of players. *Organizational Behavior and Human Decision Processes*, 38, 392–404.

Vickers, J. N. (1988). Knowledge structures of expert–novice gymnasts. *Human Movement Science*, 7, 47–72.

Vickers, J. N. (2007). *Perception, Cognition, Decision Training: The Quiet Eye In Action.* Champaign, IL: Human Kinetics.

Vickers, J. N., Livingston, L., Umeris, S. and Holden, D. (1999). Decision training: The effects of complex instruction, variable practice and reduced delayed feedback on the acquisition and transfer of a complex motor skill. *Journal of Sports Sciences*, 17, 357–367.

Vickers, J. N., Reeves, M., Chambers, K. L. and Martell, S. (2004). Decision training: Cognitive strategies for enhancing motor performance. In A. M. Williams and N. J. Hodges (eds), *Skill Acquisition in Sport: Research, Theory and Practice* (pp. 103–120). New York, NY: Routledge.

Votsis, E., Tzetzis, G., Hatzitaki, V. and Grouios, G. (2009). The effect of implicit and explicit methods in acquisition of anticipation skill in low and high complexity situations. *International Journal of Sport Psychology*, 40, 374–391.

Vroom, V. and Yelton, R. (1973). *Leadership and Decision-Making.* Pittsburgh, PA: University of Pittsburgh Press.

Walther, E., Fiedler, K., Horn, K. and Zembrod, A. (2002). Mit Siegeswille absteigen – oder mit Ballgefühl in die Championsleague? Konstruktive Gedächtnisillusionen bei Fußballexperten und -laien (To play championship soccer by flowing with the ball or to go down by trying too hard: Constructive illusions of memory in soccer experts and novices). *Psychologie und Sport, 9,* 159–171.

Wanderer, J. J. (1987). Social factors in judges rankings of competitors in figure skating championships. *Journal of Sport Behavior, 10,* 93–102.

Wann, D. L. and Schrader, M. P. (2000). Controllability and stability in the self-serving attributions of sport spectators. *Journal of Social Psychology, 140,* 160–168.

Wanous, J. P. and Youtz, M. A. (1986). Solution diversity and the quality of group decisions. *Academy of Management Journal, 29,* 141–159.

Weber, M. (1946). Politics as a vocation. In H. H. Gerth and C. W. Mills (eds), *From Max Weber: Essays in Sociology* (pp. 77–156). New York, NY: Oxford University Press. (Original work published 1919.)

Wedley, W. C. and Field, R. H. G. (1984). A predecision support system. *Academy of Management Review, 11,* 407–466.

Weinberg, R. S. and Gould, D. (2007). *Foundations of Sport and Exercise Psychology* (4th edn). Champaign, IL: Human Kinetics.

Weiner, B. (1985). An attributional theory of achievement motivation and emotion. *Psychological Review, 92,* 548–573.

Welte, J. W., Barnes, G. M., Tidwell, M. C. and Hoffman, J. H. (2008). The prevalence of problem gambling among US adolescents and young adults: Results from a national survey. *Journal of Gambling Studies, 24*(2), 119–133.

Whissell, R., Lyons, S., Wilkinson, D. and Whissell, C. (1993). National bias in judgements of Olympic-level skating. *Perceptual and Motor Skills, 77,* 355–358.

Wigton, R. S. (1996). Social judgement theory and medical judgment. *Thinking and Reasoning, 2,* 175–190.

Williams, A. M. (2008). Perceiving the intentions of others: How do skilled performers make anticipation judgements? In M. Raab, J. Johnson and H. Heekeren (eds), *Mind and Motion: The Bidirectional Link Between Thought and Action. Progress in Brain Research* (pp. 73–83). Amsterdam, Netherlands: Elsevier.

Williams, A. M. and Davids, K. (1998). Visual search strategy, selective attention and expertise in soccer. *Research Quarterly for Exercise and Sport, 69,* 111–128.

Williams, A. M., Davids, K., Burwitz, L. and Williams, J. G. (1994). Visual search strategies in experienced and inexperienced soccer players. *Research Quarterly for Exercise and Sport, 65,* 127–135.

Williams, A. M., Davids, K. and Williams, J. G. (eds). (1999). *Visual Perception and Action in Sport.* London, UK: E. and F. N. Spon.

Williams, A. M., Janelle, C. and Davids, K. (2004). Constraints on the search for visual information in sport. *International Journal of Sport and Exercise Psychology, 2,* 301–318.

Williams, A. M. and Ward, P. (2003). Perceptual expertise: Development in sport. In J. L. Starkes and K. A. Ericsson (eds), *Expert Performance in Sports: Advances in Research on Sport Expertise* (pp. 220–249). Champaign, IL: Human Kinetics.

Williams, A. M. and Ward, P. (2007). Anticipation skill in sport: Exploring new horizons. In G. Tenenbaum and R. Eklund (eds), *Handbook of Sport Psychology* (pp. 203–223). Hoboken, NJ: John Wiley & Sons, Inc.

Wilson, M. (2002). Six views of embodied cognition. *Psychonomic Bulletin and Review 9*(4), 625–636.

Wilson, V. E. (1977). Objectivity and effect of order of appearance in judging synchronized swimming meets. *Perceptual and Motor Skills, 44,* 295–298.

Wood, J., Fromholtz, M., Chapman, J. and Morrison, V. (2004). *Organizational Behavior: A Global Perspective* (3rd edn). Hoboken, NJ: John Wiley & Sons, Inc.

Würth, S., Lee, M. J. and Alfermann, D. (2004). Parental involvement and athletes' career in youth sport. *Psychology of Sport and Exercise*, 5, 21–34.

Wylleman, P., Alfermann, D. and Lavallee. D. (2004). Career transitions in sport. *Psychology of Sport and Exercise*, 5, 7–20.

Yates, J. F. (2003). *Decision Management*. San Francisco, CA: Jossey-Bass.

Yates, J. F. and Tschirhart, M. D. (2006). Decision making expertise. In K. A. Ericsson, N. Charness, P. J. Feltovich and R. R. Hoffman (eds), *Cambridge Handbook of Expertise and Expert Performance* (pp. 421–438). New York, NY: Cambridge University Press.

Yesalis, C. E. and Cowart, V. S. (1998). *The Steroids Game*. Champaign, IL: Human Kinetics.

Yetton, P. and Bottger, P. (1983). The relationships among group size, member ability, social decision schemes and performance. *Organizational Behavior and Human Performance*, 32, 145–149.

Young, T. J. and French, L. A. (1998). The 'greatest' boxers of all time: Heuristics and biases among boxing historians. *Perceptual and Motor Skills*, 87, 1310.

Author Index

Judgement, Decision Making and Success in Sport, First Edition.
M. Bar-Eli, H. Plessner and M. Raab.
© 2011 John Wiley & Sons, Ltd. Published 2011 by John Wiley & Sons, Ltd.

Indexed by Terrence Halliday

Subject Index

Judgement, Decision Making and Success in Sport, First Edition.
M. Bar-Eli, H. Plessner and M. Raab.
© 2011 John Wiley & Sons, Ltd. Published 2011 by John Wiley & Sons, Ltd.

Indexed by Terrence Halliday